KAREN CAMPBE

OFFICIAL GUIDE

HOW TO DRAW
AMAZING
HANDS

A straightforward 6 step method
for accurately drawing and shading
realistic hands in pencil.

Warning to new students:

I LIKE TO MAKE LEARNING FUN!!!
YES – EVEN WHEN DRAWING
DIFFICULT SUBJECTS... STILL FUN!

PSST...SORRY NOT SORRY!

Note to the Reader:

Hands are super hard to draw. I hope that this book serves to demystify the process and even (fingers crossed) helps make it fun! I've seen my students have great success with drawing these same gestures already.
If they can do it,
so can you YOU!

You can't get worse with more practice – that's NOT a THING!

♡ KAREN

Author, Illustrator, Publisher: Karen Campbell, Artist, LLC
www.karencampbellartist.com
Cover Layout and Design: KT Design, LLC
www.ktdesignllc.com
Editor: Linda Duvel

Table of Contents

Anatomy of the Hand

Briefly, before we go over the system I have set up for drawing hands, I want to take a quick peek at the anatomy of the hand. Every crease, every bump has a fancy, crazy-complicated, Latin name!

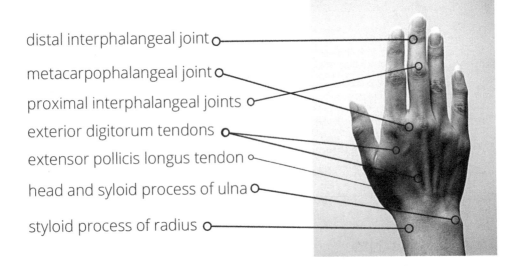

distal interphalangeal joint crease

proximal interphalangeal joint crease

metacarpophalangeal joint crease

distal transverse crease
plica interdigitalis
proximal transverse crease
radial longitudinal crease
thenar eminence
middle palmer crease
distal wrist crease
proximal wrist crease
hypothenar eminence
palmaris longus tendon

distal interphalangeal joint
metacarpophalangeal joint
proximal interphalangeal joints
exterior digitorum tendons
extensor pollicis longus tendon
head and syloid process of ulna
styloid process of radius

I don't know about you, but I am NOT going to learn about all of that (call me lazy, call me whatever you want, I'm not doing it!). To make our lives easier, I'm introducing you to my very own scientific names. These are the only terms you need to familiarize yourself with. I feel better already!

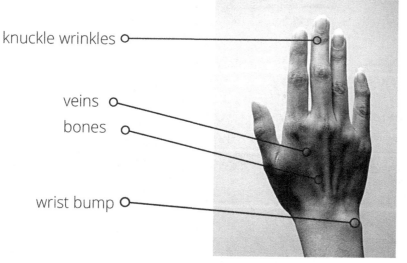

lines

elephant skin

big crease

poodge

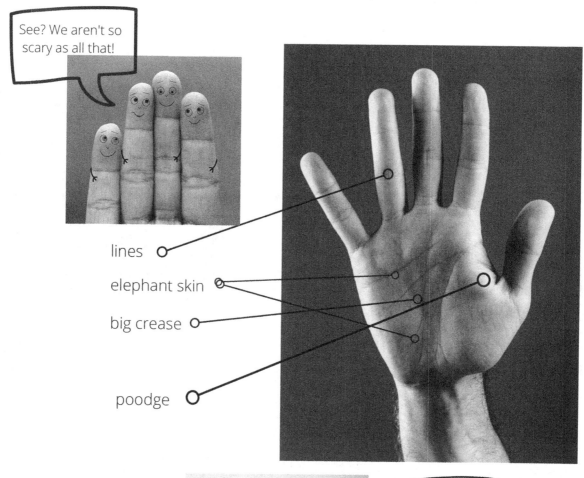

knuckle wrinkles

veins

bones

wrist bump

Mindset Shift

So the biggest take away I want you to get from this book is how important it is to see things just as black and white shapes, curves or lines. "Seeing" things correctly is literally ALL you need to be able to do to draw hands correctly! No names, no anatomy needed. Let's take those friendly fingers for example...
Instead of seeing fingers like this:

distal interphalangeal joint crease

proximal interphalangeal joint crease

metacarpophalangeal joint crease

I want you to start seeing them like this:

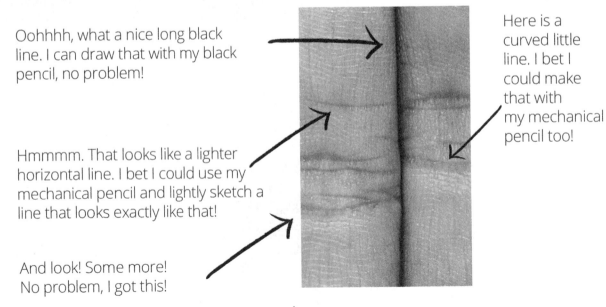

Oohhhh, what a nice long black line. I can draw that with my black pencil, no problem!

Here is a curved little line. I bet I could make that with my mechanical pencil too!

Hmmmm. That looks like a lighter horizontal line. I bet I could use my mechanical pencil and lightly sketch a line that looks exactly like that!

And look! Some more! No problem, I got this!

Let's take this one step further and actually DRAW! This is a learning book after all. Did you think you were going to get better at drawing by reading? You only get better by DRAWING so pick up a pencil (any pencil) and do this little learning exercise with me now!

Hurry! Our cute little finger family is waiting to see if you can draw them!

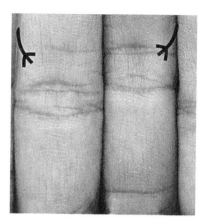

STEP 1: Draw the outline.

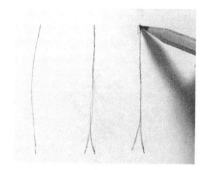

STEP 2: Add some shading using the side of your pencil.

STEP 3: Smooth out graphite with your blending stick.

STEP 4: Redraw any lost lines.

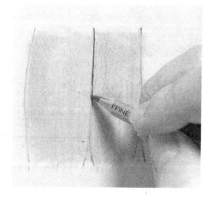

STEP 5: Try to replicate the lines you see with your pencil.

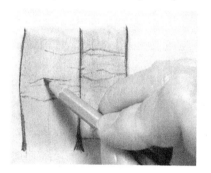

STEP 6: Blend wrinkles with tip of blending tool.

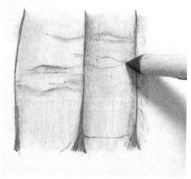

This is pretty straightforward, right? The last step is to add black. You only need to add black in a drawing if there is black in your reference photo. Chances are, there is some!

STEP 7: Add black pencil to areas that appear black on your reference photo.

More on black pencil in a few page turns!

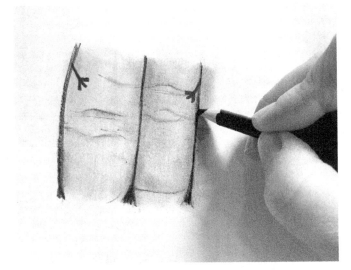

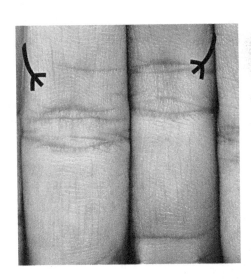
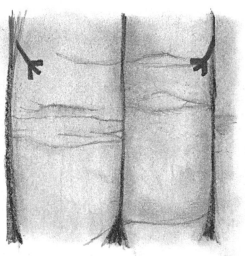

When it comes to drawing, the goal is to try and draw EXACTLY what is there before you. You don't need to understand it (fingers with hands?!), you just need to see if you can accurately copy what you see. Wee stick hands and all! The steps in this book will help you to do that easily and consistently!

8

This mindset shift is super weird at first (what do you mean a knuckle isn't a knuckle?!), but being able to see hands and fingers as just a series of lights and darks and a few weird lines (and certainly NOT an actual hand), is the key to your drawing success!

And hey look, I know what you're thinking when you see this hand...

That looks sooo hard! I can't draw that!

But if you can silence your brain (and mouth) for a hot second, let's see if you can't start to see things like this....

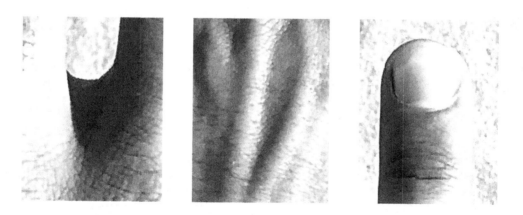

How about now? Can you see these areas are just organic shapes that have a whole range of values in them from black to white and lots of greys in between? That is literally ALL I want you to concern yourself with! Where are the blacks and greys and whites in your photo. Got it? Good, now go put them into the same places on your drawing!

9

Now let's have a turn drawing those weird veins and bones! Don't you dare groan at me, you can do this, I promise!

Remember, we don't even care that we are drawing veins and bones. We ONLY care about what we can do with our pencil to try and record what we see here. What we see here is a lot of light (even white) areas and different shades of grey (which make up the shadows). We can totally handle this! One pencil stroke at a time! I'll show you how.

STEP 1:

First of all, squint your eyes. Can you see the shapes in that photo? I sure can! Using the side of your pencil, roughly sketch in all the dark parts. Leave the white parts the paper.

→

STEP 2:

Now look at the photo again. Some of those areas are super dark, right? Using a soft pencil this time (like an 8B) color in the areas that look super dark to you.

←

STEP 3:

Blend like mad!!

10

Take a moment here to pause and look. See how much we can accomplish in only 3 steps? Were you stressing about making tendons or veins? NO! Because when we only focus our attention on the shapes and dark and light places, we know that's literally ALL we have to do! Let's move forward.

STEP 4:
In areas that you over-blend or make too dark, just erase!! So easy! I know!

STEP 5:
Look at your photo again. Need to darken up some places more? Go ahead using your soft pencil.

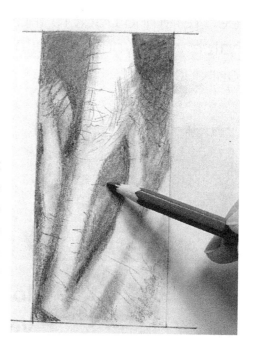

STEP 6:
Blend your heart out. Do NOT underestimate the importance of blending. It creates a seamless transition between all the shades of grey you have in your drawing. Spend as long as you need to in this stage!

Also: **DIRECTIONALITY IS IMPORTANT!**
Blending your drawing is like brushing a dog: you need to blend in the direction that the real life lines are going!

Look at the arrows to see all the different directions I had to blend my graphite in!

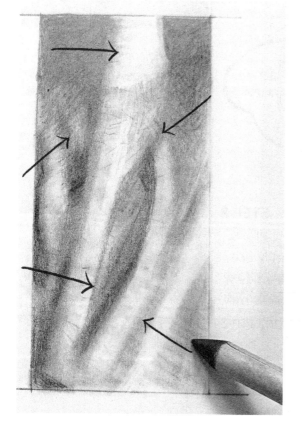

Sometimes it is necessary to dance back and forth between erasing out the light areas and adding back in the dark ones. I often have to repeat those stages (with intermittent rigorous blending!) quite a few times to get all the right shades in the right places! Just keep referring back to that reference photo and don't stop trying to match what your see with what you're drawing...no matter what your subject!

STEP 7:
When you have black in your photo, you have black in your drawing! Add that in now!

Always be looking back at your reference!

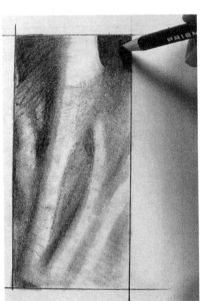

Well gosh darn. I sure do see the black and those yucky wrinkles!

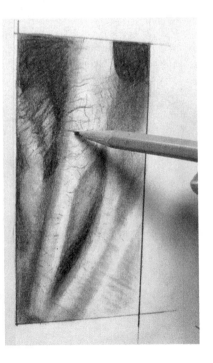

STEP 8
Details.
Got hair on there?
Draw them on! Wrinkles?
Yep, now's the time!
Just take your time and do your best!
With practice,
YOU GOT THIS!

Mine isn't perfect, but I'm okay with that. If you try your best and follow the steps outlined in this book about how to see things and in turn, how to draw them, my bet is that you'll be more than just okay. You'll be GREAT!

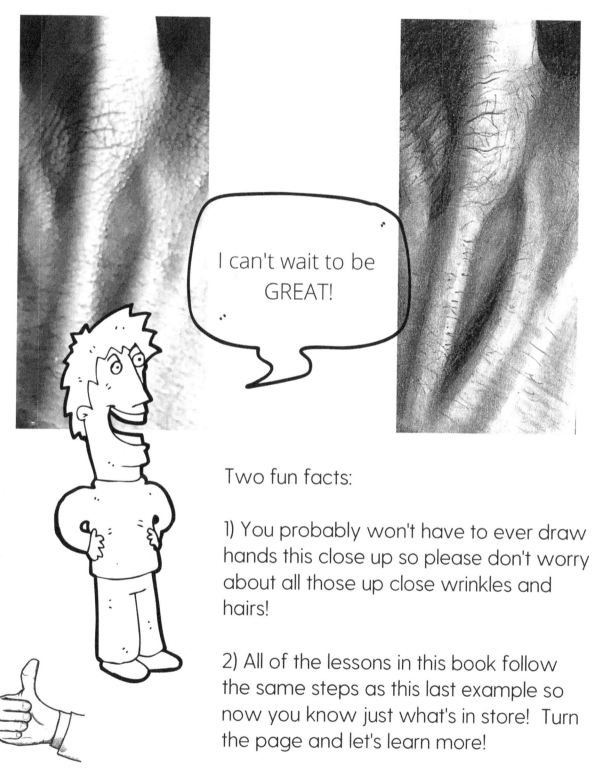

I can't wait to be GREAT!

Two fun facts:

1) You probably won't have to ever draw hands this close up so please don't worry about all those up close wrinkles and hairs!

2) All of the lessons in this book follow the same steps as this last example so now you know just what's in store! Turn the page and let's learn more!

Supply List and Value Scale

Drawing hands isn't about fancy tools; it's seeing things correctly, a boatload of practice, and the following:

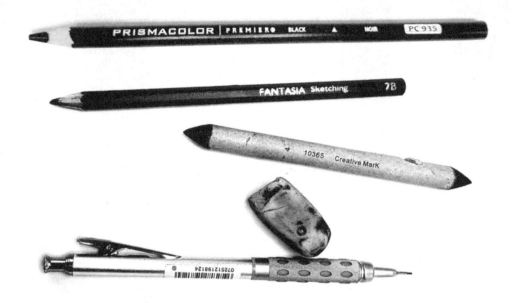

To successfully complete the exercises in this book you will need:

- Tracing paper (comes in rolls or sheets/pads)
- A sketchbook, art journal or ordinary computer paper
- A mechanical pencil. I like this weighted one from Pentel GraphGear. Use whatever you have lying around!
- A dirty blending stump
- A good eraser (or a couple). I like the Vanishing eraser or a kneaded eraser. The eraser of your mechanical pencil works really well for getting in those teeny tiny spaces!
- A soft pencil, preferably 6B or higher (the higher the number, the easier time you'll have shading!).
- A bottle of champagne so you're ready to properly celebrate your drawing wins!! (what?! Drawing hands well is a really big deal!)

Here is also a helpful breakdown of all of the values you'll need to make, and exactly what to use to make them!

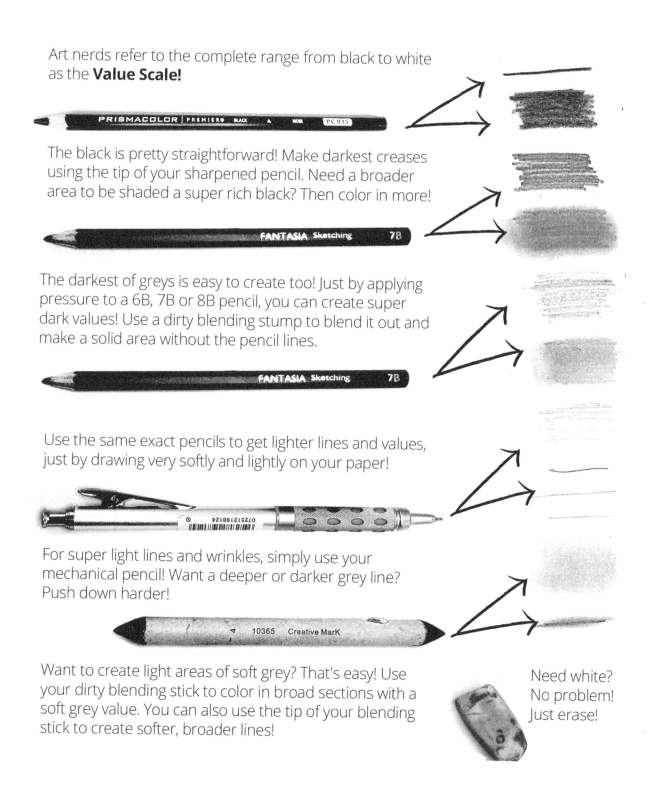

Art nerds refer to the complete range from black to white as the **Value Scale!**

The black is pretty straightforward! Make darkest creases using the tip of your sharpened pencil. Need a broader area to be shaded a super rich black? Then color in more!

The darkest of greys is easy to create too! Just by applying pressure to a 6B, 7B or 8B pencil, you can create super dark values! Use a dirty blending stump to blend it out and make a solid area without the pencil lines.

Use the same exact pencils to get lighter lines and values, just by drawing very softly and lightly on your paper!

For super light lines and wrinkles, simply use your mechanical pencil! Want a deeper or darker grey line? Push down harder!

Want to create light areas of soft grey? That's easy! Use your dirty blending stick to color in broad sections with a soft grey value. You can also use the tip of your blending stick to create softer, broader lines!

Need white? No problem! Just erase!

Still wondering what all the fuss is about? Still not seeing the value of the Value Scale?

Well, using ALL the values (so a touch of all greys, from light to dark PLUS black and white) makes for a much more dynamic and powerful drawing effect!!

It's easiest to see when you look at two examples side by side:

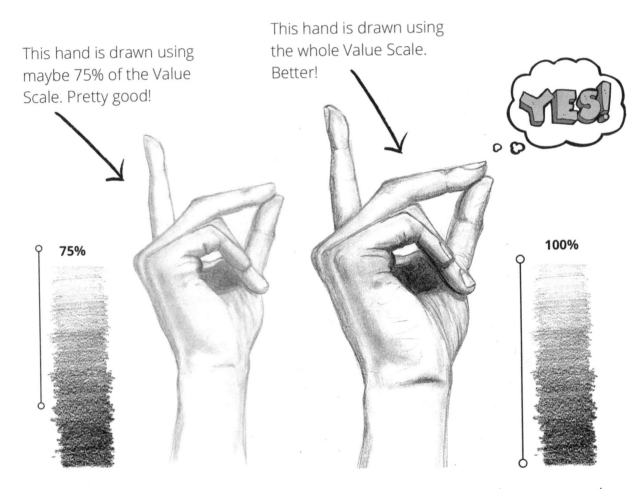

This hand is drawn using maybe 75% of the Value Scale. Pretty good!

This hand is drawn using the whole Value Scale. Better!

75%

100%

YES!

Higher contrast equates to more dramatic results! Is the one on the left wrong, nope. But does the one on the right look just a little bit more realistic and interesting? I would argue, Yes! This is, of course, my own personal preference. If you love the softer look of graphite without the black, you do you! Art is all about personal expression and creating what looks and feels good to you, so do what you like!

6 Step Process

Black and White Photographic Reference of Hand

Why no color?
Hands are HARD to draw. Black and white photos give us clear cut information that we can use to make amazing drawings. This book will teach you how.

Tracing paper (you'll need at least 3 sheets per hand).

1

First we will lay our trace over the photo and take our time tracing the outline of the whole hand and fingers. This helps us develop the muscle memory that will make us better artists.

2

With the second sheet of trace, we will color in the negative spaces around the fingers and any unusual places or shapes that we see. I'll explain as we go why this is so important.

3

The third time we trace we will be paying attention to relationships between things, angles, and lines (straight or curved).

4

After collecting information, analyzing the shapes and practicing our drawings on trace, it is time to draw! We will start with just the outline.

5

Once the outline is perfected (this is the hardest part), we will add shading with our soft pencils and blend.

6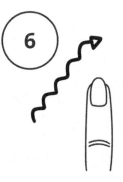

Lastly, we add details like fingernails, wrinkles, knuckle bumps and all the other weird little details that often go on hands! Add black pencil where needed.

Tracing the Outline

This book will teach you how to draw hands from scratch. However, I fully acknowledge that drawing the outline of the hand can be really tricky, even for experienced artists! To make drawing the outline easier, feel free to trace them. Use graphite transfer paper to accomplish this; it's easy! Transfer paper is widely available online and at your local arts and crafts store.

STEP 1: Lay the photocopy of the hand you wish to draw on top of your drawing paper.

STEP 2: Slip the transfer paper between your photocopy and your drawing paper. Make sure that the DARK (graphite) side is DOWN.

STEP 3: Using a sharp drawing utensil, trace the outline of the hand.

STEP 4: Lift your transfer paper and photocopy to reveal the outline drawn for you!

Note about Muscle Memory: Since hands and their positions can vary so incredibly widely, it is very difficult to build muscle memory when drawing them, unless you're drawing the same position over and over again. With this in mind, tracing the outline when drawing hands can help build your confidence and encourage you to **draw even more**. Practice is THE most important thing when trying to become better at drawing so if tracing helps you overcome initial difficulties of getting started then I encourage you to do so!

I can tell you right off the bat that there is no easy or hard hand to draw. They are all a challenge in their own way. I do want to start off with at LEAST a more light hearted activity, so let's start off with this peace sign. In this first example I will reveal all the steps, techniques, tips and tricks to make every single hand drawing in this book. I will keep the original photo reference and subsequent tracings and drawing attempts at exactly the same scale so that you can see exactly what to do and how to do it.

The remaining lessons will be a bit more concise, with fewer steps, simply to keep the book from becoming a million pages long. If you ever need to revisit a tip, specific technique or stage, know that you can always refer back to that fun "peace out" project to jog your memory and give you back the confidence you need to continue on!

Peace Out

Here we go! When choosing a reference photo for your drawings do yourself a favor. Choose a photo that has high contrast (so lots of black and white and everything in between).

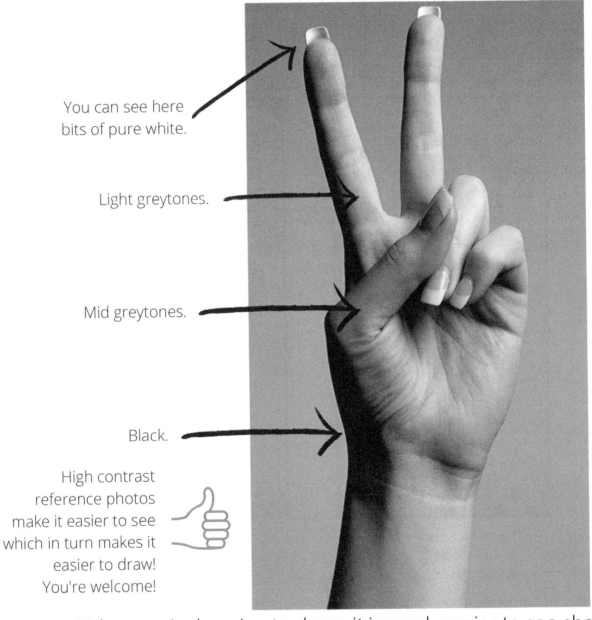

You can see here bits of pure white.

Light greytones.

Mid greytones.

Black.

High contrast reference photos make it easier to see which in turn makes it easier to draw! You're welcome!

When you're learning to draw, it is much easier to see shading and highlights, midtones and nuances, when you DON'T also have to deal with color. That's a different bag a worms and trust me when I tell you, we have our hands full with the worms we got right here!

20

When you get to the reference photo in each lesson, take a photocopy or a scan of it and then take it back to your desk. I will always keep the first photo reference nice and large so you can even trace it from the book if you prefer. Use three pieces of tracing paper each and get ready for the warm up.

Psst...scan or trace me!

21

1

First we will lay our trace over the photo and take our time tracing the outline of the whole hand and fingers. This helps us develop the muscle memory that will make us better artists.

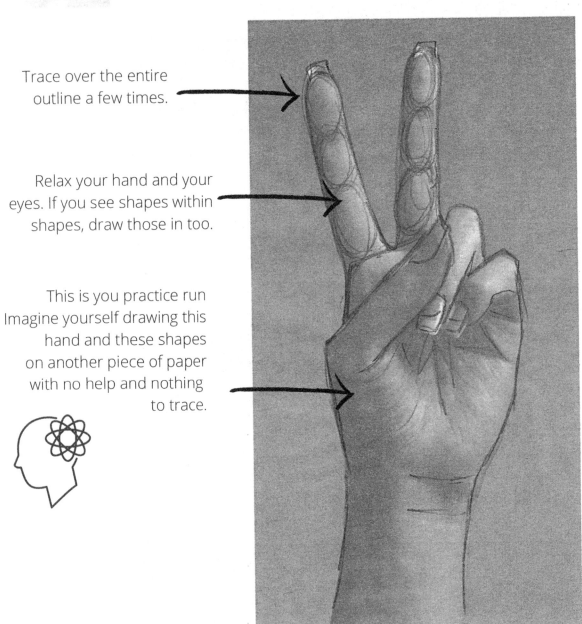

Trace over the entire outline a few times.

Relax your hand and your eyes. If you see shapes within shapes, draw those in too.

This is you practice run Imagine yourself drawing this hand and these shapes on another piece of paper with no help and nothing to trace.

Scared? Me too! That's why we take our time and trace this over and over until we are bored and feel ready to move on to step 2.

2 With the second sheet of trace, we will color in the negative spaces around the fingers and any unusual places or shapes that we see.

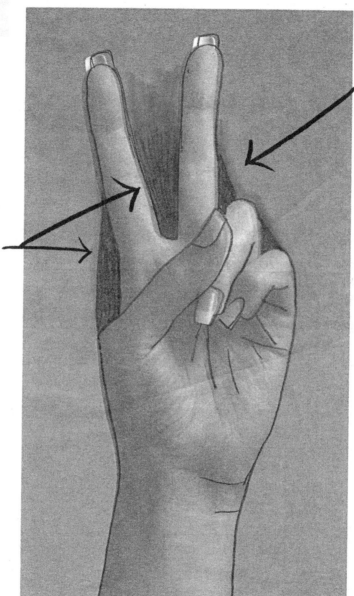

Check out these "V" shapes. There are TONS of those in your hand-drawing future!

Just you wait!

Make this fun for yourself! A coloring page for adults! Section off the weird outside shapes and shade them in.

I am still keeping this in the same scale as the original.

See how those negative spaces pop out at you? This becomes an important measuring device by which we can see if our own original drawing is on track! This step also forces us to see the hand in terms of simple shapes ONLY. Simplifying how we view the hand helps make drawing easier and less overwhelming.

23

3 The third time we trace we will be paying attention to relationships between things, angles, and lines (straight or curved).

I write little notes to myself to remind me of the important details

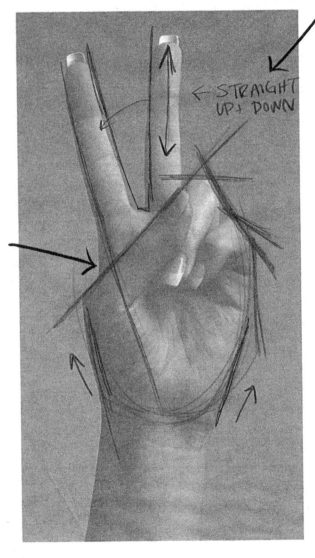

← STRAIGHT UP↓ DOWN

Sweeping directional guidelines are very helpful too. You are not just noting them here. You are practicing them and building important muscle memory too!

Feel like you're still not ready to move on? Then don't! Grab yet another piece of tracing paper and trace as many times as you want. This isn't a race, it's just learning and it's okay to take your time.

Directional arrows are helpful. They remind me of the angles I need to try and reproduce on my own paper later!

Hands are just so complex, by taking the time to deconstruct them, we can put them back together in our own drawings in a more understandable way. At least that is the hope!

4  After collecting information, analyzing the shapes and practicing our drawings on trace, it is time to draw! We will start with just the outline.

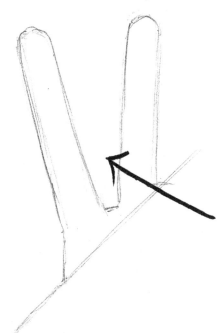

Start out very very slowly.

Draw just one or two fingers.

Then check your work against your original traces!

I'm already wondering if I have that angle right between the two fingers. Good thing I have my negative tracings to check it against!

Start out drawing with your mechanical pencil. The precision tip keeps sharp which means you don't have to waste time stopping to sharpen it. Lord knows, we have enough to do!

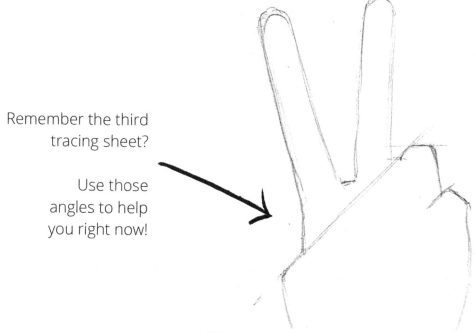

Remember the third tracing sheet?

Use those angles to help you right now!

4 Step 4 continues as I stop and check the lines I have drawn so far against my second (negative space) tracing.

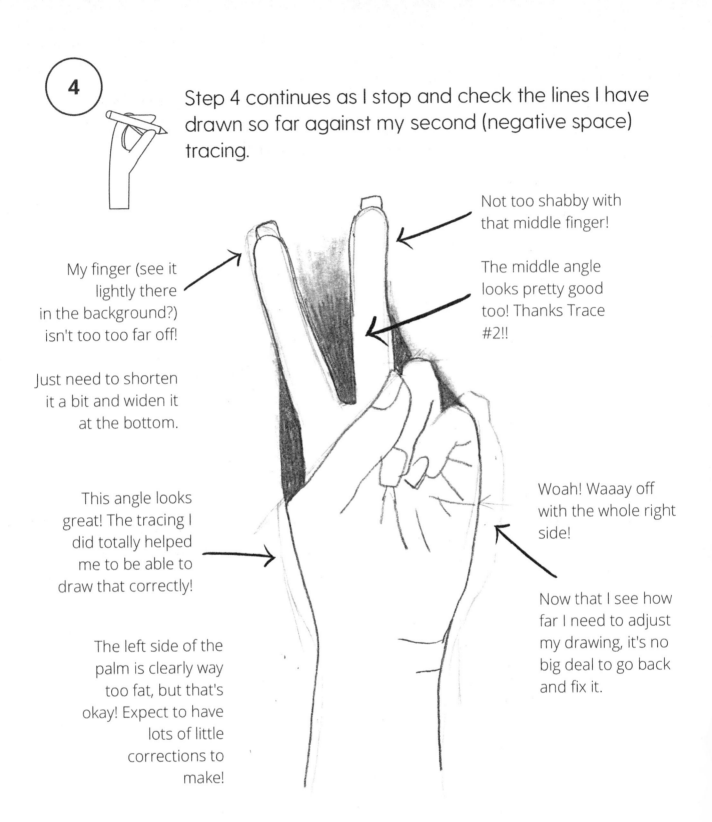

Not too shabby with that middle finger!

The middle angle looks pretty good too! Thanks Trace #2!!

My finger (see it lightly there in the background?) isn't too too far off!

Just need to shorten it a bit and widen it at the bottom.

This angle looks great! The tracing I did totally helped me to be able to draw that correctly!

The left side of the palm is clearly way too fat, but that's okay! Expect to have lots of little corrections to make!

Woah! Waaay off with the whole right side!

Now that I see how far I need to adjust my drawing, it's no big deal to go back and fix it.

Woah! I was way off!! But now I know. I go back to my original drawings and tweak the lines to make them as close as possible to the photo reference.

4 Step 4 (for me at least) is the most work intensive. Just take your time and go around to each part of the fingers and hand, tweaking the angles, bumps and relationships so that your final outline matches your tracing outlines. That is all we are setting out to do here.

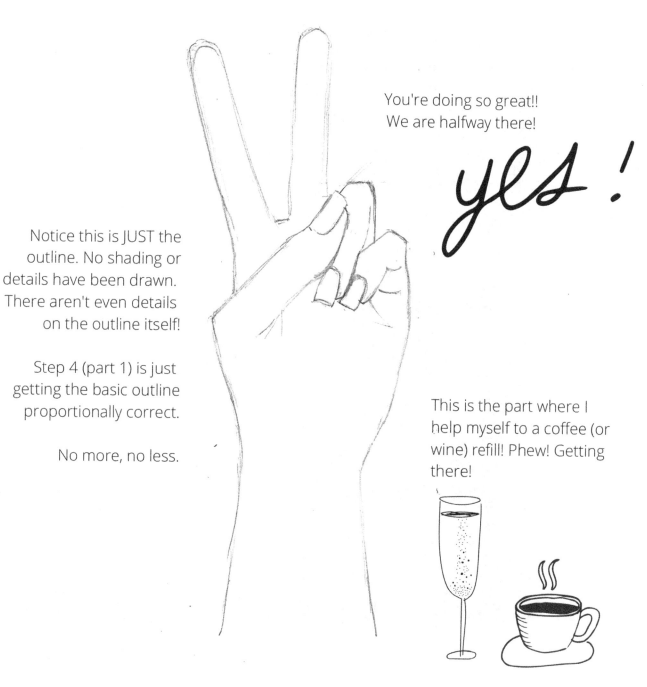

You're doing so great!! We are halfway there!

yes!

Notice this is JUST the outline. No shading or details have been drawn. There aren't even details on the outline itself!

Step 4 (part 1) is just getting the basic outline proportionally correct.

No more, no less.

This is the part where I help myself to a coffee (or wine) refill! Phew! Getting there!

4 Finally, we can wrap up step 4. At this stage I painstakingly go around my entire reference photo and note anything and everything pertaining to the outline that I can't leave out and try to capture that in my drawing. That includes things like…

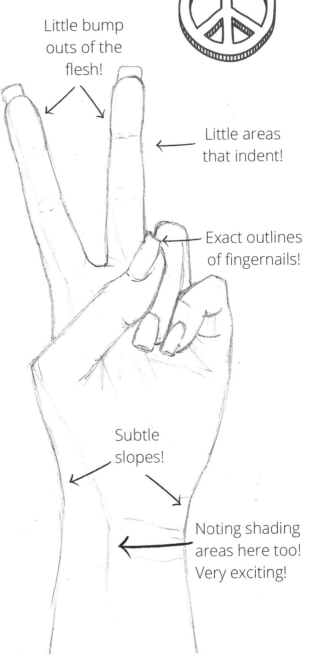

Little bump outs of the flesh!

Little areas that indent!

Exact outlines of fingernails!

Subtle slopes!

Noting shading areas here too! Very exciting!

5 I never thought this day would come! FINALLY! Once the outline is perfected (this is the hardest part), we will add shading with our soft pencils and blend. Step 5 is all about shading. I have LOTS of tricks and tips for this section so pay close attention!

When shading, use the SIDE of the softest pencil you own!!

Rub graphite lightly onto your paper by keeping the tip almost PARALLEL to the paper!

HOT TIP!

Psst...Still to scale!

5 Not sure where to shade? The BEST part about working in black and white (or pencil/graphite) is that there is no guessing. Just pull out your reference photo and do what it tells you to do!

You ask:
So...this part is SUPER white...does that mean that will be white when we're done?

Me: yes

You ask:
So...this part is black...does that mean that will be black when we're done?

Me: yes

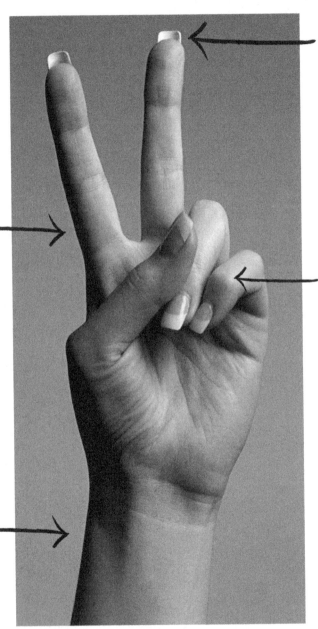

You ask:
This part is kinda greyish (but light), I feel like if I brush just a little of my pencil there it'll make a similar really light shade of grey...is that the right way to do it?!

Me: yes

You ask:
Oh man. That shaded region practically makes a whole shape in and of itself! Am I supposed to try and make that on my drawing too? With just my pencil and blending stump? Try to make it look the same?

Me: yes

Have confidence with shading!
You know all that you need to know
(and way more than you THINK!).

life is good

30

5 Start blending with your dirty blending stump at the darkest areas. Slowly work the graphite out into the areas that aren't as dark. Then gently ease your blending stump from the middle value (middle greytone) until it fades out into the lightest areas.

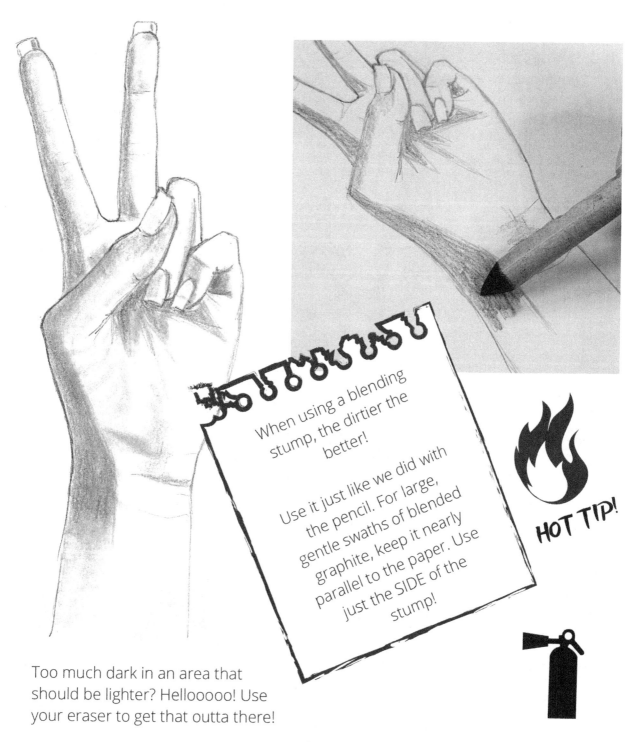

When using a blending stump, the dirtier the better!

Use it just like we did with the pencil. For large, gentle swaths of blended graphite, keep it nearly parallel to the paper. Use just the SIDE of the stump!

HOT TIP!

Too much dark in an area that should be lighter? Hellooooo! Use your eraser to get that outta there!

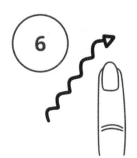

6 Lastly, we add details like fingernails, wrinkles, knuckle bumps and all the other weird little details that often go on hands! Add black pencil as needed.

Once again, not sure where to go? Refer to that awesome reference photo and add in all the deets you see from there.

Shading on fingernails?! If you see it in your reference photo then put 'em in there!!

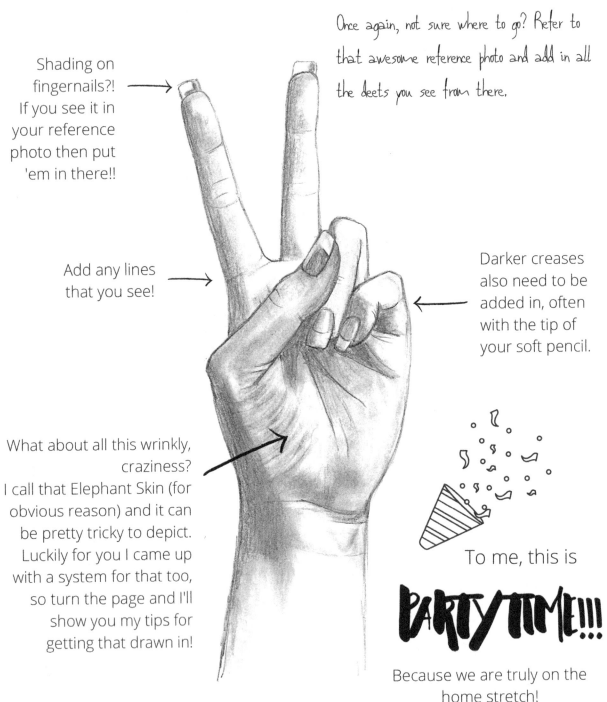

Add any lines that you see!

Darker creases also need to be added in, often with the tip of your soft pencil.

What about all this wrinkly, craziness? I call that Elephant Skin (for obvious reason) and it can be pretty tricky to depict. Luckily for you I came up with a system for that too, so turn the page and I'll show you my tips for getting that drawn in!

To me, this is

PARTY TIME!!!

Because we are truly on the home stretch!

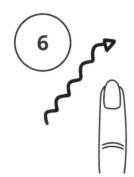

6 Capturing the wrinkly and bumpy portions of the palm sometimes takes quite a bit of back and forth between your pencil, blender, and eraser. This wrinkled part is the Elephant Skin I keep mentioning. Unfortunately, It appears on a lot of hands! No use fighting it, let's learn how it's done.

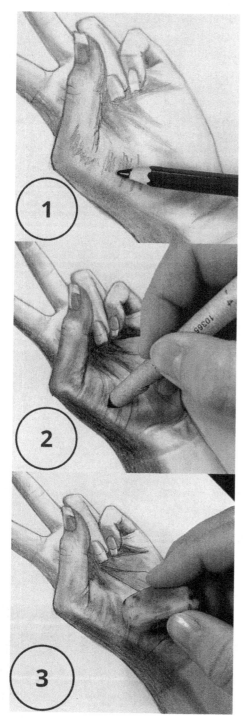

1 First, apply a light layer of graphite using the side of your pencil (just like we did for basic first shading areas).

NOTE: It important to keep your pencil lines going in the same direction as the wrinkles on the skin!

2 Now take your blending stump and using the TIP of it this time, blend the graphite back and forth (in the same direction as the wrinkles).

Using the tip of your blending stump (rather than the side) accentuates the lines and makes them come across as deep creases (which is good!!).

3 If there is now too much graphite down and the area looks too solid (and elephant skin is clearly not solid, but wrinkly and strange), simply take your eraser and lightly erase out portions of the graphite.

33

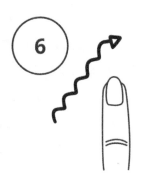

6 Try experimenting with different erasers to get different effects. You can sometimes "carve" out highlighted areas much more easily than you can try to draw around them with shading!

"Pouncing" a large eraser will gently lift off larger areas of graphite on your paper. Great for palms and larger wrist sections or the broad, back of hands!

Pouncing is just a term that means repeated dabbing. You can apply light pressure or hard pressure, depending on how much graphite you are trying to lift

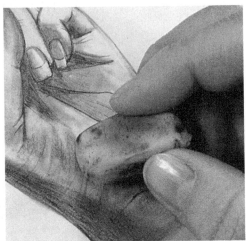

Using the side of my Blackwing Pencil eraser I can easily make long, white highlighted, wrinkly areas with practially no effort at all!

OMG drawing with my eraser is literally, SO AWESOME.

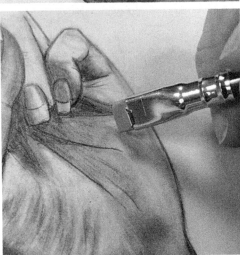

No need to invest in specialty erasers to get into small spaces (although if you want to, the Mono Eraser by Tombow is excellent!).

The small eraser at the end of my Pentel Graphgear mechanical pencil gives me all the power I need to carve out amazing highlights and to correct tiny mistakes!

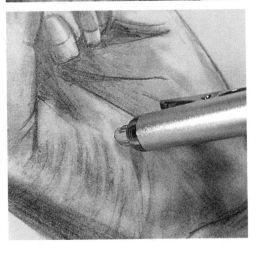

6 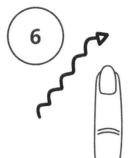 The very last step after all the details have been added and all the white parts have been carved away by the eraser, is to softly and slowly add black colored pencil to the very darkest shaded areas of the drawing.

There's usually not too much black to add either! Just around the left hand side and in the dead center of the palm area. Make sure you blend the black pencil (just by applying soft pressure) into the dark grey graphite, so that there isn't a harsh line between the values.

AND DONE!

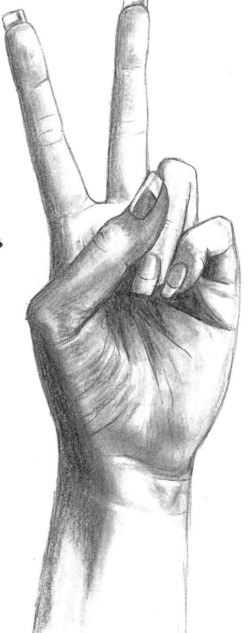

The Alien

I never thought a hand, by itself, could have character, but when I saw this hand gesture that's all I could think of! It reminds me of some cute little alien cartoon character! I totally enjoyed drawing this one (especially that bizarre Poodge!) and I really hope that you do too!

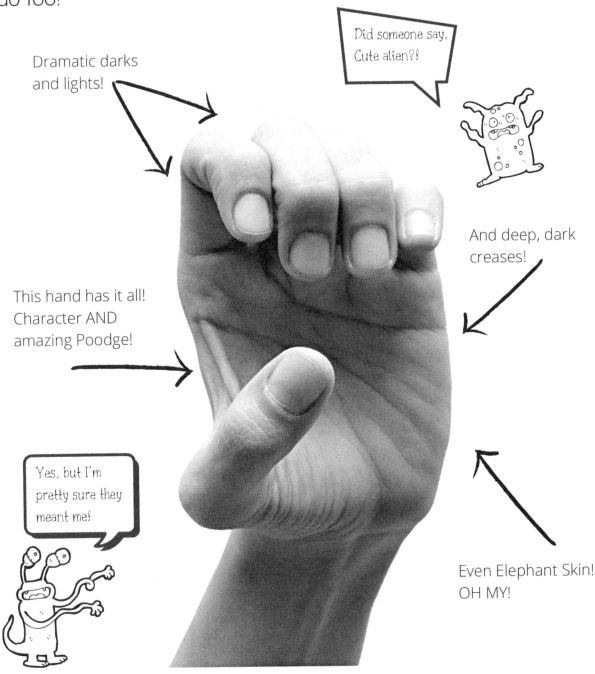

Dramatic darks and lights!

Did someone say, Cute alien?!

And deep, dark creases!

This hand has it all! Character AND amazing Poodge!

Yes, but I'm pretty sure they meant me!

Even Elephant Skin! OH MY!

1

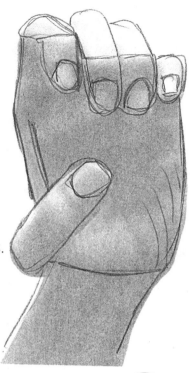

Use your first trace to block out the overall basic shapes.

2

The triangular shapes between the knuckles, Poodge and wrist area help perceive those relative angles.

3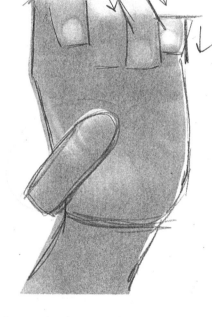

Speaking of angles...your third trace should focus on the directionality of those fingers. Each one is going in a different direction! Note that on your paper.

37

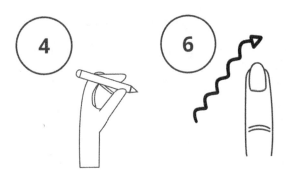

Due to the fact that there is so much happening in this gesture, it is a good idea to draw in the fingernails before we go ahead and start the shading.

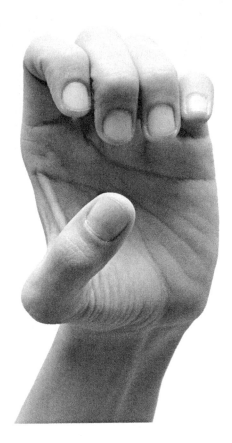

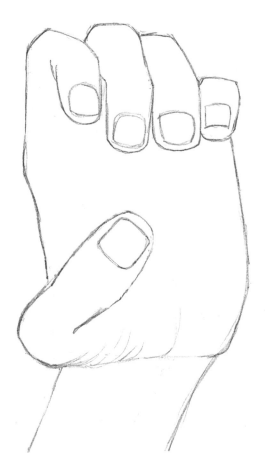

It is also okay to start on the fingernails in this case because they are mostly all highlighted, so it makes sense to "preserve" the whites of the nails in this case, rather than to shade them and then have to erase them out later.

Still struggling to freehand the outline? Don't stress over it too much! Use the instructions on page 18 to help you transfer the outline. This gesture is 10% outline and 90% shading magic so let's focus on the shading details as that's really what matters.

5 There is a LOT happening with the shading in this one so let's take this one step at a time. First, put down a good amount of graphite from your soft pencil everywhere that is shown here.

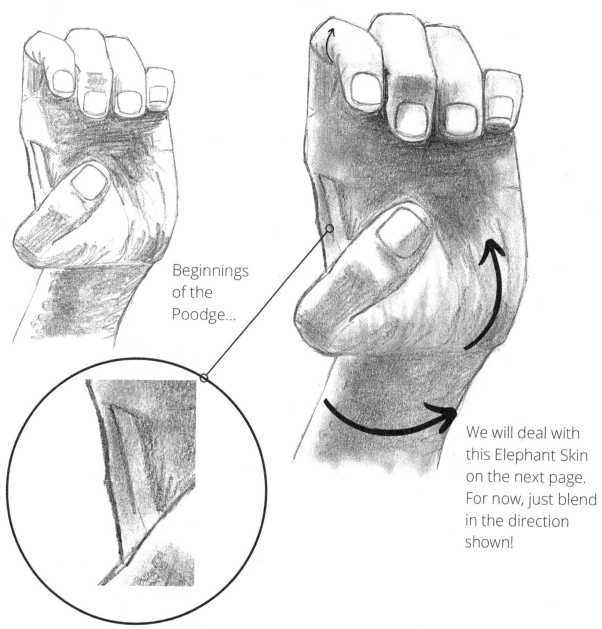

Beginnings of the Poodge...

We will deal with this Elephant Skin on the next page. For now, just blend in the direction shown!

Then, using your blending stump, as dirty as you can make it, and blend all of that graphite around. Make sure to pay close attention to the directionality of your blended areas. Refer to the areas and the arrows above to help guide you! Not sure of where to blend? Follow the wrinkles! They will tell you where to go!

5 So begins our deep-dive into the beloved Elephant Skin again! As always, we will take this step by step. Follow these steps and, with practice, you're hands will start to look more and more realistic!

Step 1: Lay down a nice first layer of graphite and blend in the direction of the skin (we already did that in the previous page.)

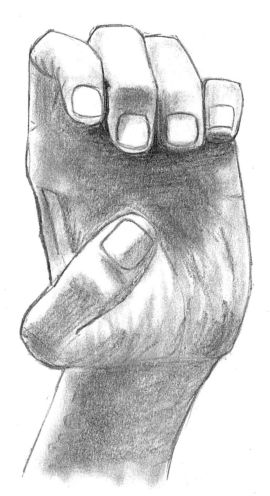

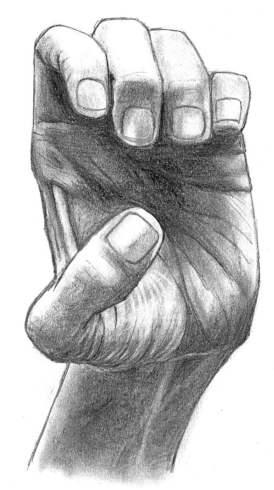

Our goal is to go from this,   to this.

5 So many hand gestures have Elephant Skin. The more you draw it, the better you'll be at mastering it! Let's continue.

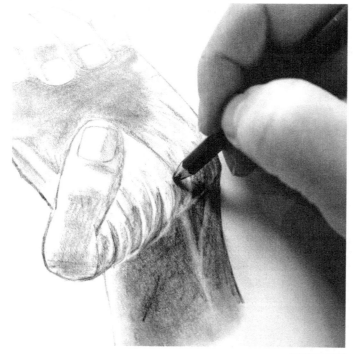

Step 2: With your softest pencil, make short pencil strokes from the base of the palm, up towards the center.

The directionality is key here, so make sure you are drawing your lines in the same upward swooping direction that you're blending them in. Follow the direction of the wrinkles in the skin if you are unsure!

 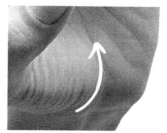

Step 3: With the back of your mechanical eraser, erase out lines in the same sweeping directions as your pencil strokes in Step 2 and your blending strokes in Step 1.

Once again, you got this! Elephant Skin is crazy but it's totally doable!

5 This drawing (and Elephant Skin) is a bit more involved than the Peace Out gesture. Just keep following the steps. You got this!

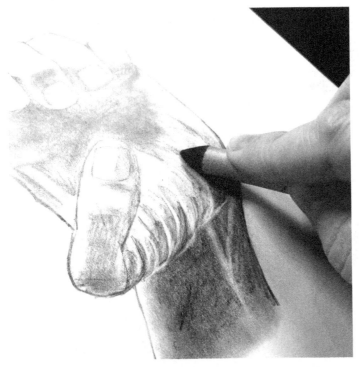

Step 4: Now, with your dirty blending stump, LIGHTLY blend out, all of the pencil and eraser marks you just created in the previou steps.

Make sure, as always, that you blend in the exact same directions as the wrinkles and creases appear in the original reference photo.

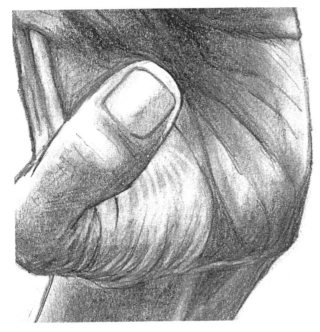

Step 5: Repeat as often as necessary to produce the desired Elephant Skin effect!

Sometimes you will carve out too much white, like here. If that's the case, you just blend it over a bit more with your stump.

Too blended? Lost the white? Go back to Step 2 and add a touch more graphite with your soft pencil. Blend again.

It is normal to have to dance between Steps 2 and 4 quite a few times inorder to get the right balance of white and blended graphite. Take your time; it's not a race!

5 Now that we have successfully created our Elephant Skin, let's see how awesomely and easily we can deal with this strange "Poodge" area.

Step 1 Draw an outline, as best as you can, of the Poodge area. To review, the "Poodge" is the weird, stretchy patch of skin that exists between the forefinger and thumb.

Step 2 Blend around the two little parallel lines. Make sure that the areas above and around the 2 lines are darker than the space between the lines.

Step 3: Add more graphite around the parallel lines again (no photo shown).

I'm having flashbacks to the beginning of the book where we drew the close up of the man's hand. Remember that? This is a very similar situation where it is of utmost importance to not think too hard about what's happening with the skin. You simply take in the shapes and darks and lights as they appear, and do your best to record only THAT specific information onto your own paper. No less, no more. You got it? Awesome! Let's continue.

The "Poodge" development continues!

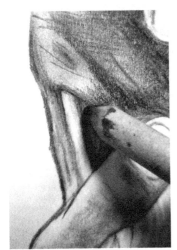

Step 4 Blend again with any yummy, dirty, blending stump.

Step 5 With a small eraser, create a stronger highlight by erasing a line down the middle of the 2 parallel lines.

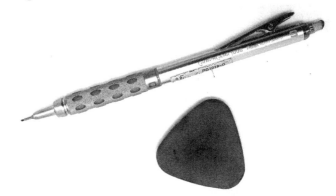

Step 6 Accentuate the look of the 2 parallel lines (the heart of the "Poodge") by adding a touch of darker graphite to the corner areas.

Refer to the original photo to see exactly where those areas are.

Remember: All the information you need about lighting and shading are contained in your reference! When in doubt, check it out!

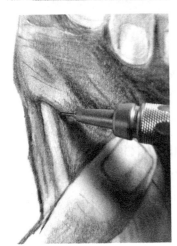

After that Elephant Skin and Poodge giant tangent, we need to finish up the hand as a whole. To recap, we had the outline and beginning shaded stages complete.

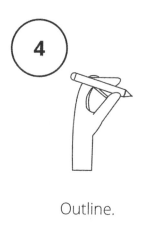

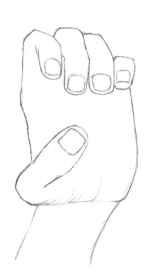

Outline.

First layer of graphite put down.

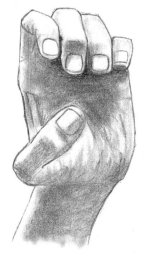

Blend up all the graphite..

Here is where the refining starts.

Add a second layer of graphite to the mid palm.

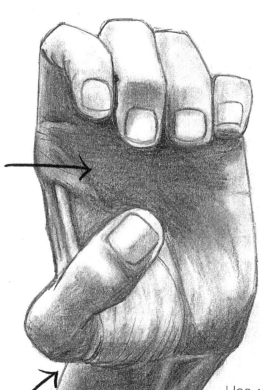

Also add it to the darkest parts of the fingers and wrist.

Use eraser to highlight Elephant Skin, Poodge and wrist bones.

45

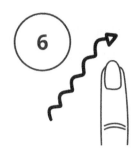

6 To add the dark creases and wrinkles that accentuate this awesome hand, in an area that is already deeply shaded, use a wide nib mechanical pencil with a bold graphite. I love to use my .9 Pentel GraphGear 1000 and a lovely 2B lead for occasions such as this.

And last but not least, for that added drama, use a bit of black pencil for the darkest, blackest depths of that shadowy inner palm area!

We want you!

Does this not remind you of that old "Uncle Sam wants YOU" poster? Couldn't resist this challenge and I'm sure there are so many great instances where knowing how to draw this gesture could be a lot of fun!

Sweet! Grab my leash!

After the Elephant Skin and Poodge of the last hand, this one will feel like a walk in the park! Woot, let's go!

As always, make sure you take the time to analyze the forms, angles, negative spaces and relationships of the hand parts before you attempt to draw anything.

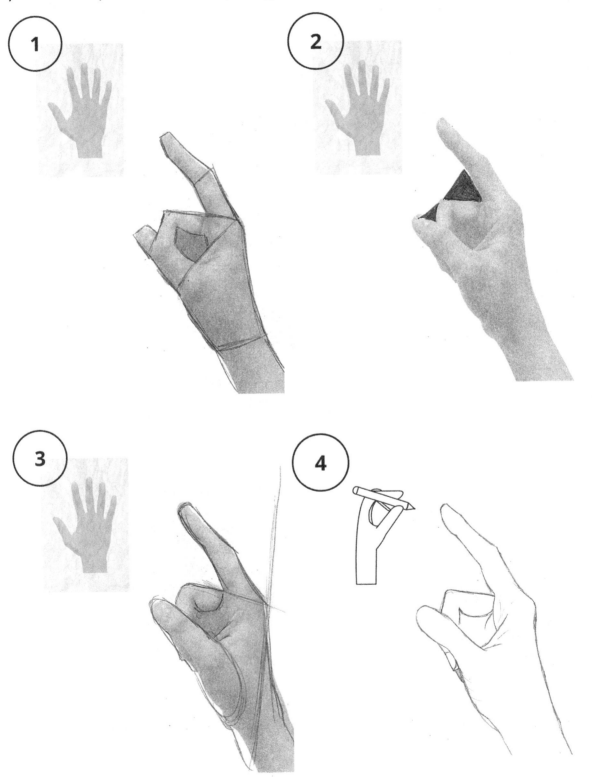

5 The shading on this hand isn't dramatic, but like anything you draw that you want to make look three dimensional, careful attention must be made to the darkest areas!

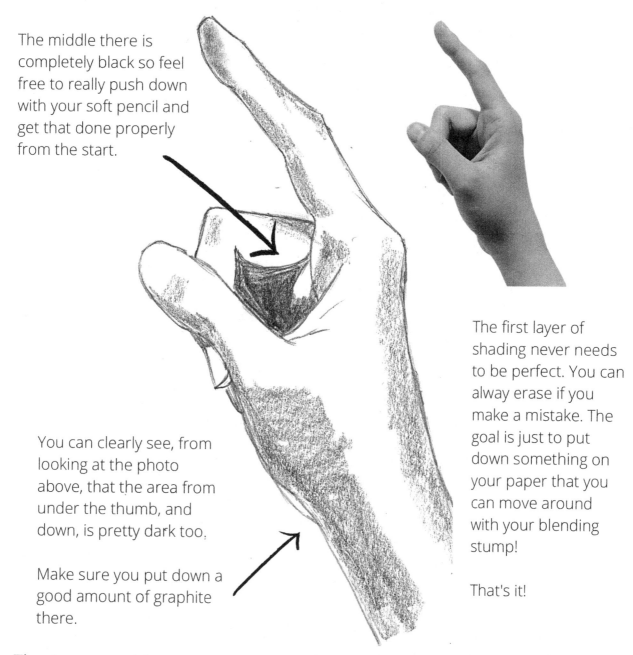

The middle there is completely black so feel free to really push down with your soft pencil and get that done properly from the start.

You can clearly see, from looking at the photo above, that the area from under the thumb, and down, is pretty dark too.

Make sure you put down a good amount of graphite there.

The first layer of shading never needs to be perfect. You can alway erase if you make a mistake. The goal is just to put down something on your paper that you can move around with your blending stump!

That's it!

The two most important times to look at your reference photo are when you're drawing the outline and when you begin shading. Look for the overall darkest regions and start there.

5

In any given hand drawing, you should be spending more time blending than drawing or erasing. This is especially true when you get to the advanced stages of shading. Really concentrate on making sure that there are darker areas and lighter shaded areas. If you need to "lift" a larger area because of too much graphite, it's perfectly okay to "pounce" that area lighter with a larger eraser.

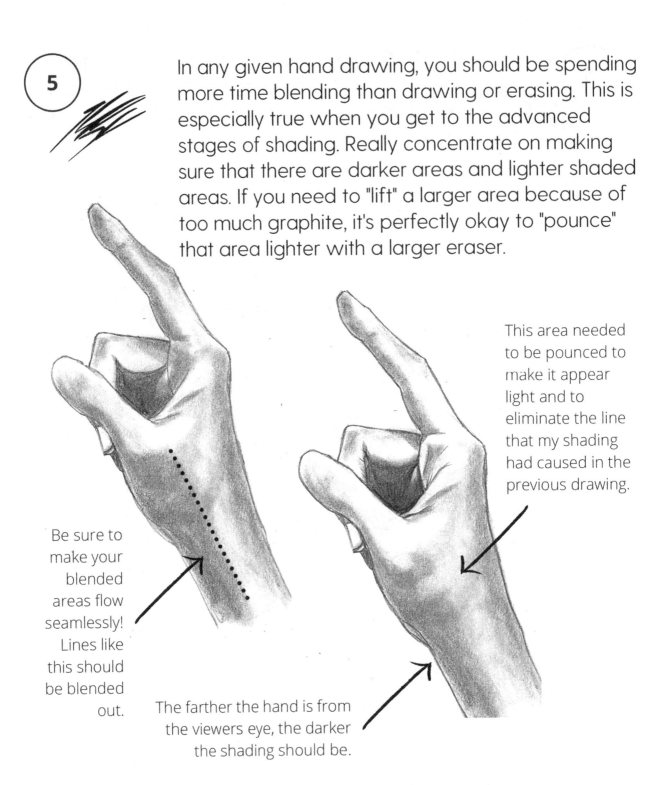

This area needed to be pounced to make it appear light and to eliminate the line that my shading had caused in the previous drawing.

Be sure to make your blended areas flow seamlessly! Lines like this should be blended out.

The farther the hand is from the viewers eye, the darker the shading should be.

Add a second pass of graphite in areas that need to appear darker. With your pencil, experiment with pressing down harder and softer to see the difference in the mark making effect it has. The better you know your tools, the better outcome your drawing will have!

5  Sometimes details are drawn in, and sometimes they are erased out! The wrinkles that make up the Elephant Skin at the base of the thumb were created using a fine tipped eraser. The effect is much more realistic.

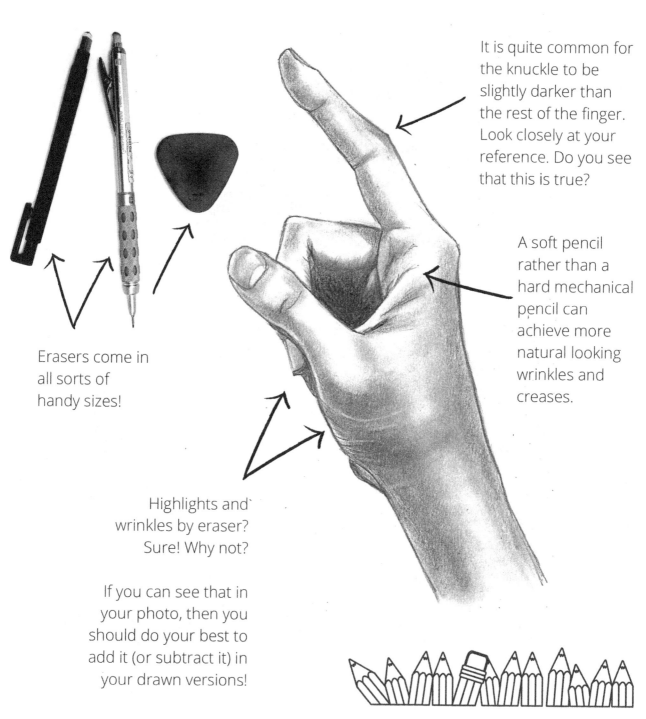

It is quite common for the knuckle to be slightly darker than the rest of the finger. Look closely at your reference. Do you see that this is true?

A soft pencil rather than a hard mechanical pencil can achieve more natural looking wrinkles and creases.

Erasers come in all sorts of handy sizes!

Highlights and wrinkles by eraser? Sure! Why not?

If you can see that in your photo, then you should do your best to add it (or subtract it) in your drawn versions!

 # Zombie

Make sure you make a photocopy of this hand, or trace right over the image in the book. Remember not to skip those first tracings! They are everything!!!

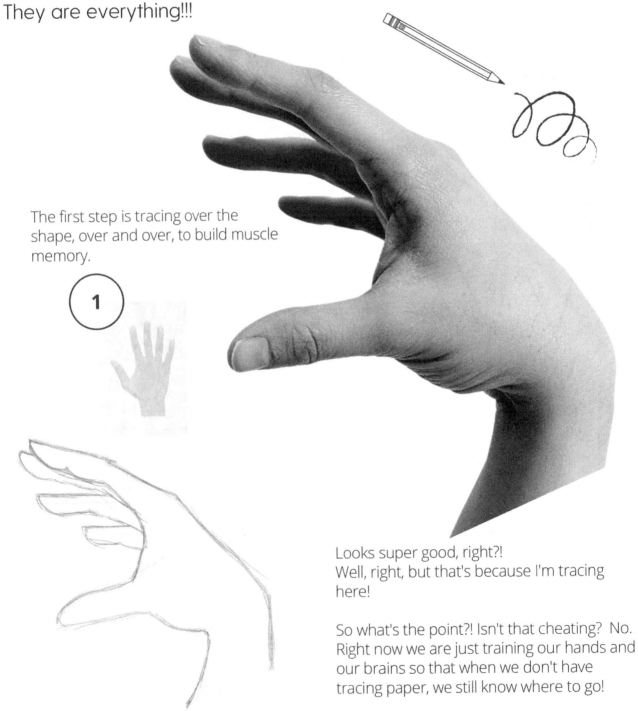

The first step is tracing over the shape, over and over, to build muscle memory.

1

Looks super good, right?!
Well, right, but that's because I'm tracing here!

So what's the point?! Isn't that cheating? No. Right now we are just training our hands and our brains so that when we don't have tracing paper, we still know where to go!

52

(2)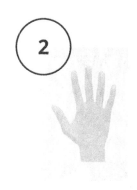

Things to note while you're tracing:
- What is the relationship between the fingers? Are they touching each other? Overlapping?
- What is the negative space between all the fingers?

Take a few moments and shade in the negative space around the fingers. Pay close attention to the distance between the fingers and the shape of the negative space around them.

As previously discussed, negative space is the empty space around and between the objects you are drawing. Notice that negative space has a shape all it's own!

You can use the negative space shape you're drawing to check that everything is in the right place when you get your final drawing done.

If you've done the final drawing correctly, the negative space of the photo reference should (theoretically) match the negative space of your final drawn version!

Great job!

3 Start another tracing.
This time, draw the general shapes of the hand. Draw a large overall shape for the bulk of the palm area. Now draw large oval loops over the large segments of the fingers.
Note the size relationships that jump out at you.

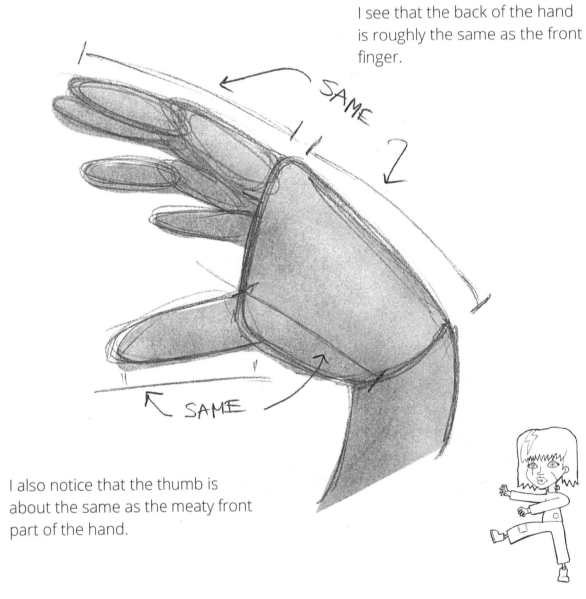

I see that the back of the hand is roughly the same as the front finger.

SAME

SAME

I also notice that the thumb is about the same as the meaty front part of the hand.

Now when you begin your final version, you can aim to make those relationships the same!

3 Feel free to do as many tracings as you like! You could do a 4th and pretend that you are sitting down with your clean sheet. Start drawing (and tracing) using the new proportions you have just noted, and the negative space that we were paying attention to. Practice gliding your pencil along the curves of the fingers and the hand and imagine you are drawing without the aid of the photo underneath. Practice these lines again and again. Leave all your lines in and don't erase. Just draw and notice relationships, over and over.

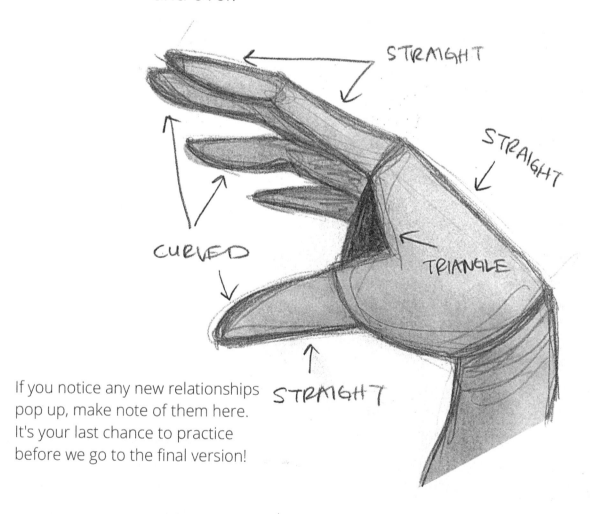

If you notice any new relationships pop up, make note of them here. It's your last chance to practice before we go to the final version!

This is so exciting!! We are almost ready!

4 Now it's time to start drawing on a fresh sheet of paper. Don't forget to set that timer for five minutes. Don't make these drawings your life's work. The object is to capture the information that your reference gives you, record it on your tracing papers, and then regurgitate that same information onto a blank sheet.

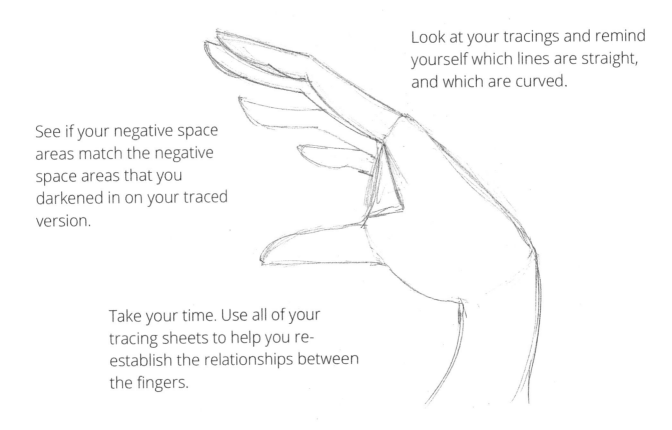

Look at your tracings and remind yourself which lines are straight, and which are curved.

See if your negative space areas match the negative space areas that you darkened in on your traced version.

Take your time. Use all of your tracing sheets to help you re-establish the relationships between the fingers.

This time, feel free to erase as much as you need to. We aren't concerned with any details at this point, ONLY the main regions of the hand and fingers. Make sure all the lines that are supposed to be straight are straight here. Make sure that all the lines that are curved, are curved in the right way. Do fingers need to be thinner? Fatter? Is that triangle in the middle still there and then same size as in your traced version? Tweak this as much as you need to until your overall shape matches the overall shape of your photo reference.

4 Really take your time and fine tune the overall outer shape of the hands and fingers. Are there little weird bump outs here and there that you didn't see before? Add those in here. The skin tends to get weird and lumpy between the thumb and wrist, and again between the thumb and forefinger. See if you can try to draw that in here. Again, just the outline of it. Then erase all extraneous lines.

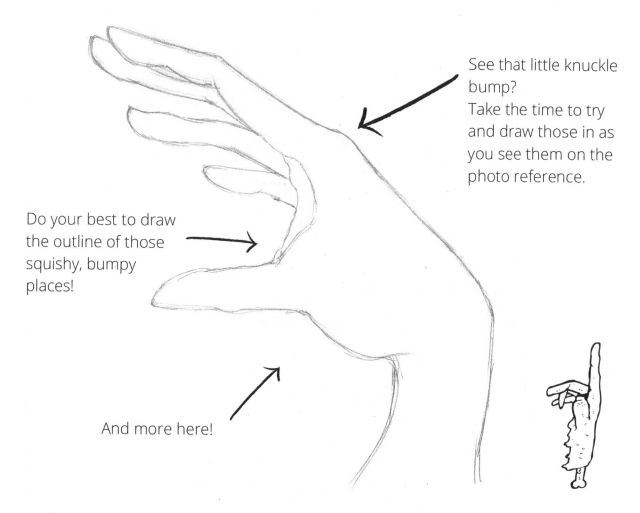

See that little knuckle bump?
Take the time to try and draw those in as you see them on the photo reference.

Do your best to draw the outline of those squishy, bumpy places!

And more here!

Note we are not dealing with any detail on the skin yet. This final stage is JUST about getting the overall outline of the hand drawn correctly. Once that is finalized, we can move onto the fingernails, wrinkles and shading! Shading first!

5 Now we can add some shading! Horray! We are getting there! With a soft pencil (I am using a 7B here) start to add graphite in the dark areas of the hand.

No black and white reference? Then squinting your eyes can be helpful to see the darker values.

I find it easier to shade my drawings when I'm using a black and white reference. That is why this book is in black and white!
To make it easier for you!

Just drawing the darker areas would look like this.

Now, using a dirty blending stump or even just a Q-tip, spread the graphite around until it looks something like this.

Next stop, wrinkles and nails!

6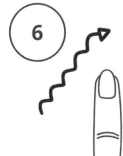

No slowly go around to each section of the hand, finger by finger, and add in wrinkles, folds and fingernails as you see them.

Any zombies need a trim? Anyone?

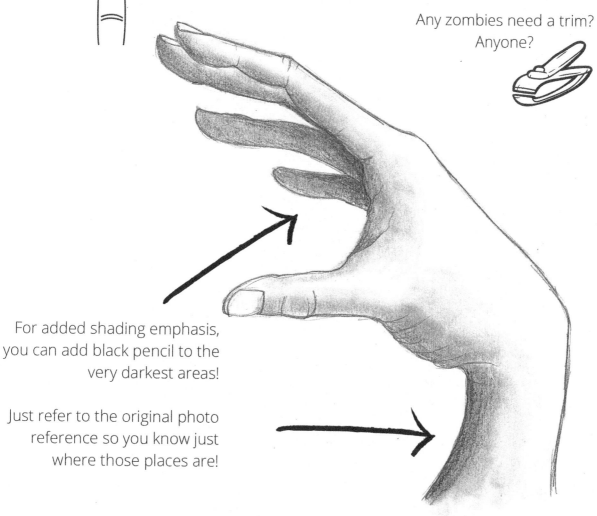

For added shading emphasis, you can add black pencil to the very darkest areas!

Just refer to the original photo reference so you know just where those places are!

If you need to erase the fingernail shading because the nail is lighter than the skin, feel free to do so! CONGRATULATIONS! You've done it!

 # Bang Bang

Okay this time I want you to draw every single step with me! Get out your tracing paper and pencil and let's begin! Here is our reference.

Use this exact image and lay your tracing paper on top. Now follow me!

1 Get out your tracing paper and
pencil and let's begin!

First time you trace,
take the time to note the
overall shapes!

2

Now, using a new
sheet of trace, color in
the negative spaces.

3

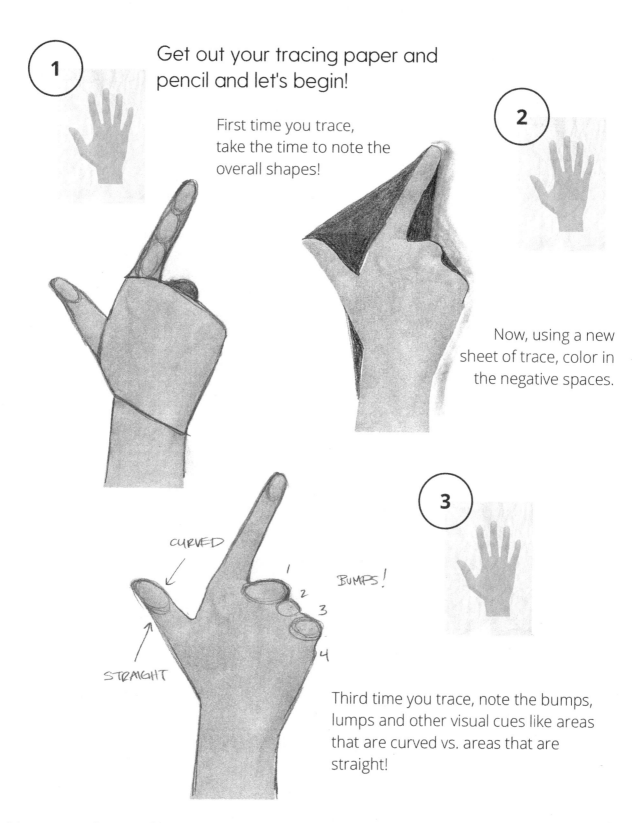

CURVED

STRAIGHT

BUMPS!

1
2
3
4

Third time you trace, note the bumps,
lumps and other visual cues like areas
that are curved vs. areas that are
straight!

Now you have three sheets of tracing paper that have lots of
important information about how to draw this hand. Let's see if we
are ready to grab a fresh sheet of paper to begin drawing.

4 Use this first tracing sheet to draw the outlines of the hand. This gives the most amount of information that you need to get started.

First time you trace, take the time to note the overall shapes!

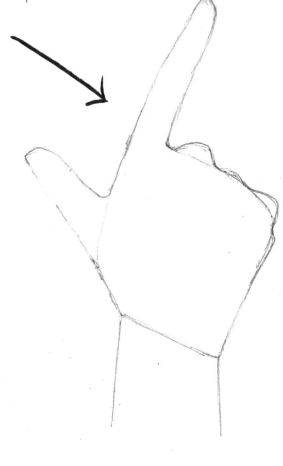

If you find you get stuck on the angle of that forefinger...

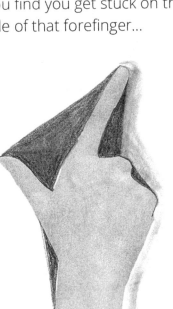

Use the angle from your negative space drawing to help correct it.

Because you have 3 traces of your hand so far, you can also lay those tracings over your final drawing to see how close you are!

5 Once you have the angle of the forefinger corrected, you can finalize the very outer-most line of the hand and erase any extra lines. Then you can add some shading using our soft B pencil.

Remember to use the original reference photo to determine which areas are darker.

And if you can't use a black and white image, squint your eyes to see the lighter and darker values more easily!

Use the side of your soft pencil and not the tip, to get nice, soft areas of graphite..

It's the easiest to determine where shading goes when you use references that are in black and white. Here, I'll make it easier for you!

63

Now blend the shaded areas with your dirty blending stump.

Use the side of your blending stump instead of the tip (just like we did with the pencil, remember?) to make lovely, soft shaded areas.

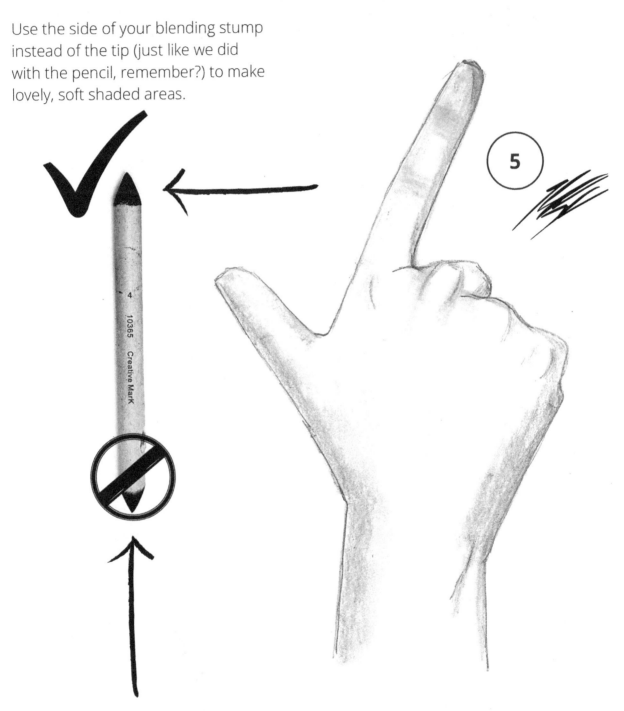

Slowly work your way around the whole hand, adding graphite and blending it softly, wherever you see it on your reference photo. Too much shading? Not a problem, simply erase!

Now it's time for the details! Add in the fingernails, wrinkles and lines!

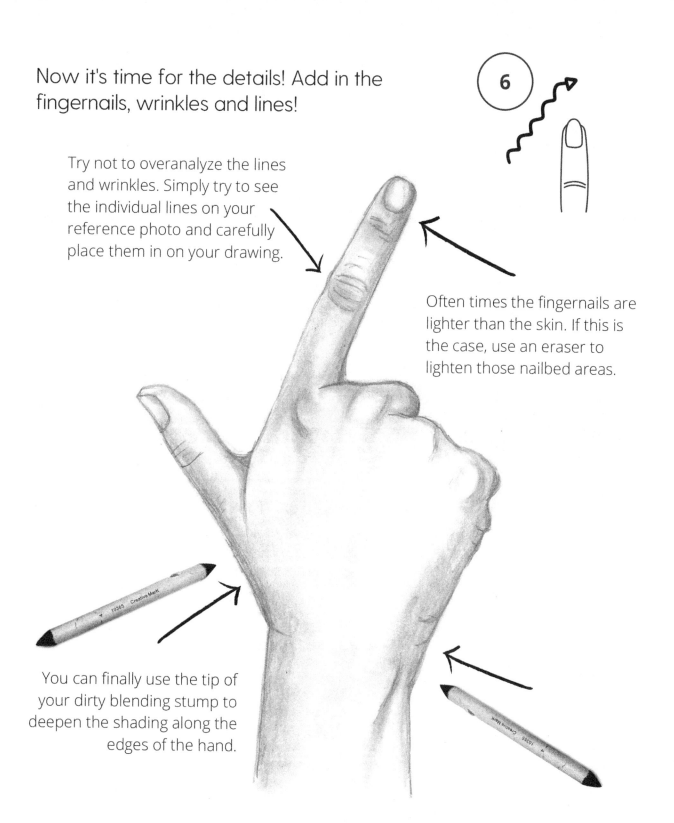

Try not to overanalyze the lines and wrinkles. Simply try to see the individual lines on your reference photo and carefully place them in on your drawing.

Often times the fingernails are lighter than the skin. If this is the case, use an eraser to lighten those nailbed areas.

You can finally use the tip of your dirty blending stump to deepen the shading along the edges of the hand.

Congratulate yourself on a job well done!! You DID IT!! You will be following this same system on each hand here so grab your tracing papers and meet me on the next page!

The Dancer

I'm excited to bring to you this graceful (and easier) hand position!

My brain is already looking for patterns, is yours?

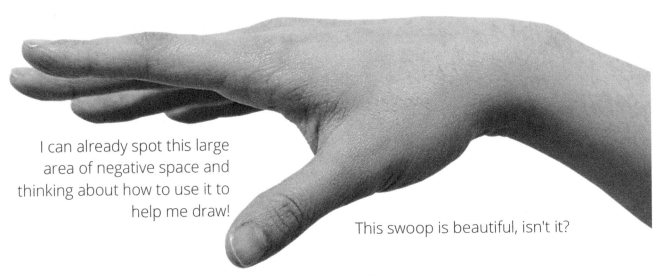

I can already spot this large area of negative space and thinking about how to use it to help me draw!

This swoop is beautiful, isn't it?

Grab 3 sheets of tracing paper and let's get this party started!

This angle is especially important because it is commonly found in fashion and figure drawings. My next book will be on drawing fun, fab figures! Master this hand here and you'll be one step ahead!

Let's get this party started with our tracings as usual! It can very helpful to write down the curves and straight parts. It helps you to pay extra close attention to all the parts of the hand before you have to draw it.

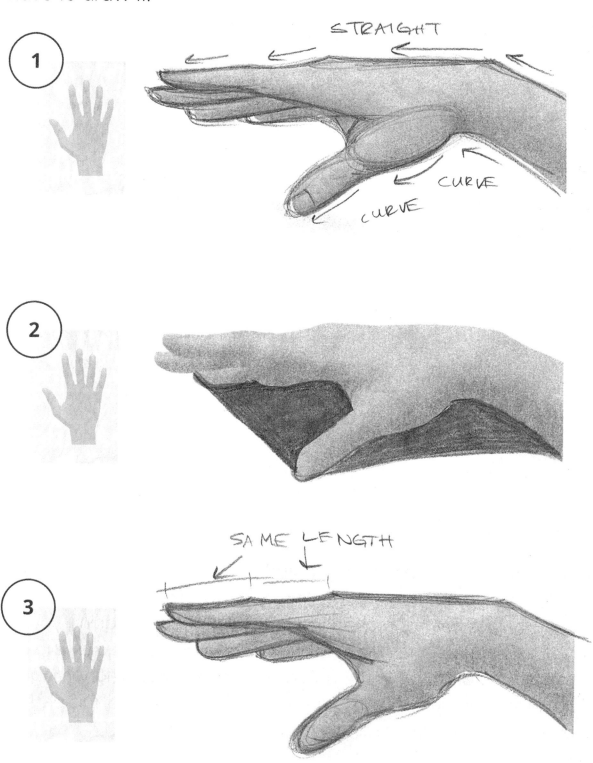

3 Cont.

By the time you've done 3-4 tracings, hopefully you'll be ready to put pencil to paper, for real!

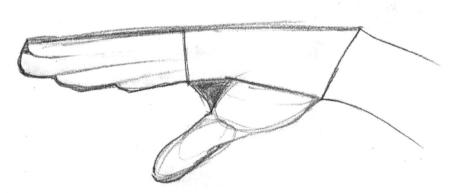

If you take your time with your tracings, the hope is that they really will help you to draw quite successfully after just a few attempts!

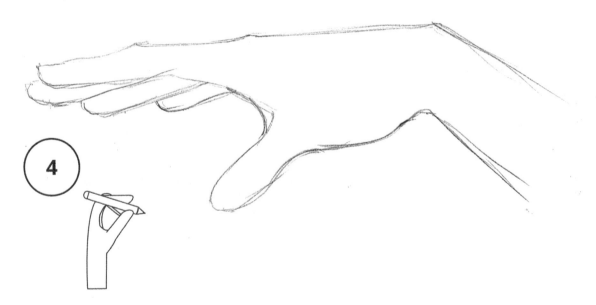

4

You can use the tracing paper studies to check your work as you go! This is so incredibly helpful, feel free to take advantage of that! The tracings are not a cheating tool, as you're not tracing your final drawing. Rather, they are a way to track your successes, line by line, as you draw on your final sheet of paper. Nothing wrong in having a little guidance as you go! And, as discussed, it is perfectly okay to transfer the outline as well.

5 You can start laying down some graphite in the darkest areas as soon as you are done with the outline.

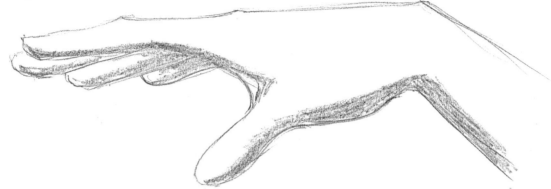

And then begin to blend.

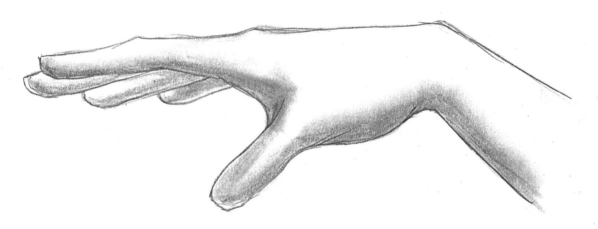

Remember to keep your photo reference nearby!

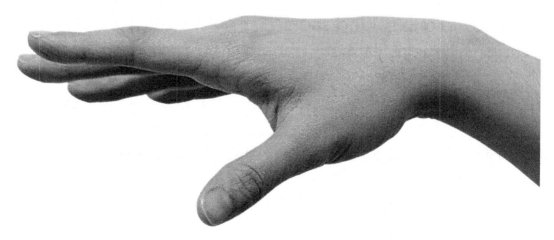

I love this part! Work your eyes around the hand and slowly start adding in the fingernails, wrinkles, knuckles and other little details!

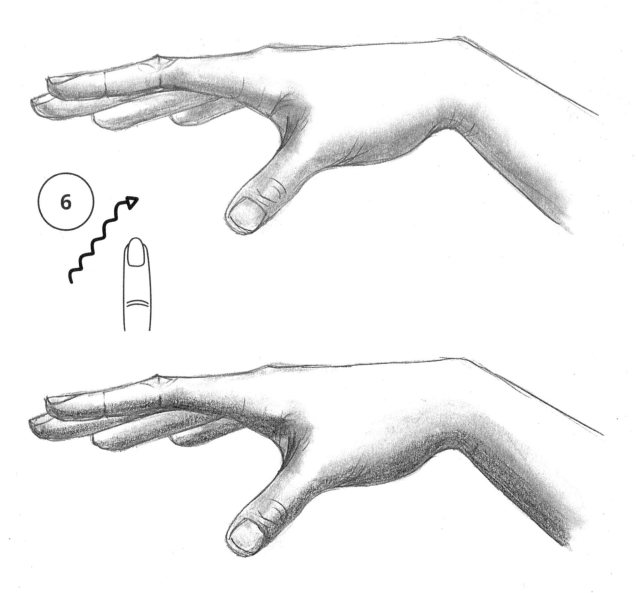

For the final touch and added shading drama, go around the shaded regions and added a bit of black colored pencil. It's really helpful to use the entire value scale when drawing anything! Remember, using the whole value scale just means that you are using every value from white to black. You can't get black with a regular graphite pencil. Only black can give you black! Just a touch adds extra depth and dimension. Plus it's so so easy to do, so why not?

One More Thing

Get your trace or transfer paper ready and then let's go!

I think you know what to do this time! I cannot stress enough how important it is to for you to take your time and go through all of these tracing practices!

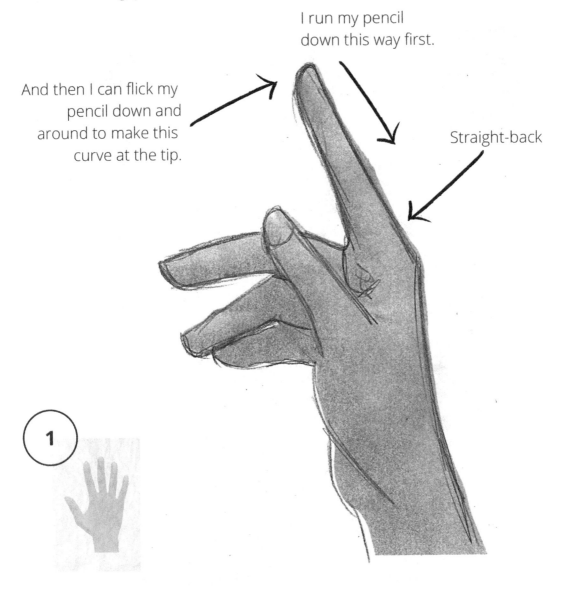

I run my pencil down this way first.

And then I can flick my pencil down and around to make this curve at the tip.

Straight-back

If you're doing these hands in order, you've done quite a few already!! You should (hopefully) be getting better at making that transition from straight back to curve, at the tip of each finger! It's exciting!

THAT is how you build muscle memory: practice and repetition!

I never tire of staring at the negative spaces. I love how the different shapes force my brain to see this hand and my drawing as something entirely different and new! I hope this is helpful for you too.

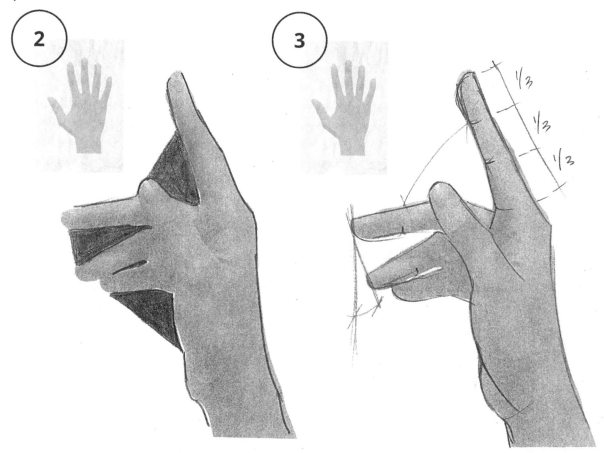

Make sure that all of your tracing attempts capture different information. One session is just to build muscle memory, and another helps you notice angles, measurements and the relationship between the fingers, distances and whether a line is curved, bumpy or straight.

Personally, I find that just noticing all of these things BEFORE I pick up my pencil to draw, makes me much more efficient and capable of drawing the hand, or any subject for that matter. It reminds me of prepping and priming a wall before painting where 90% of the work is in the prep! Drawing hands, for me, feels very similar to this!

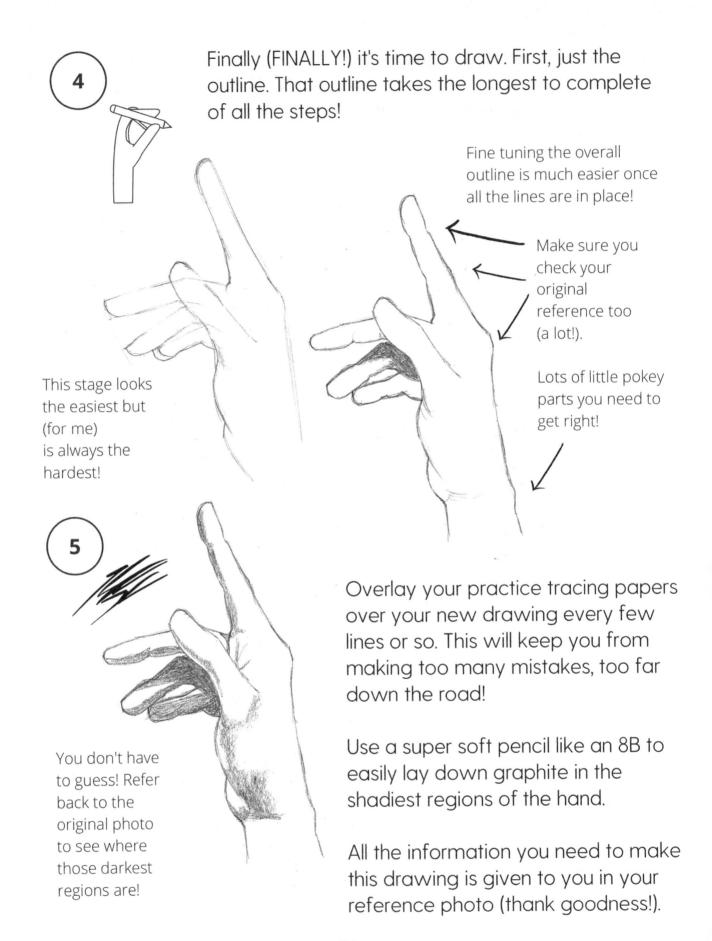

4 Finally (FINALLY!) it's time to draw. First, just the outline. That outline takes the longest to complete of all the steps!

Fine tuning the overall outline is much easier once all the lines are in place!

Make sure you check your original reference too (a lot!).

This stage looks the easiest but (for me) is always the hardest!

Lots of little pokey parts you need to get right!

5 Overlay your practice tracing papers over your new drawing every few lines or so. This will keep you from making too many mistakes, too far down the road!

Use a super soft pencil like an 8B to easily lay down graphite in the shadiest regions of the hand.

You don't have to guess! Refer back to the original photo to see where those darkest regions are!

All the information you need to make this drawing is given to you in your reference photo (thank goodness!).

Oh happy days! Blending time! Sometimes it seems counter-intuitive to blend before the details go on. My view is, we have enough to deal with, don't we? Let's take our time and just focus on one thing at a time. We'll get there, I promise (25 times to be exact!).

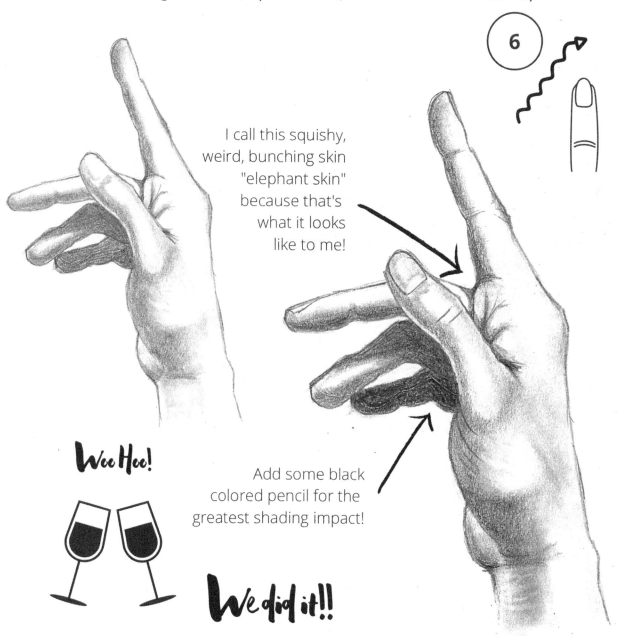

I call this squishy, weird, bunching skin "elephant skin" because that's what it looks like to me!

Woo Hoo!

Add some black colored pencil for the greatest shading impact!

We did it!!

Slowly trace over each and every millimeter of every finger and hand part with your eyes, and then your pencil! Add in any nails, forgotten bumps, wrinkles, knuckle creases, darker shading, any tiny minute detail we may have left out. Then celebrate for goodness sakes! This is hard work and you've earned it!

Fisty-Cuffs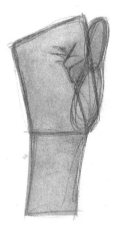

1-3

A little Elephant skin in this one and hey! Only one finger! A new and exciting form to trace for starters. Following the same process for each hand, your tracings should look something like this.

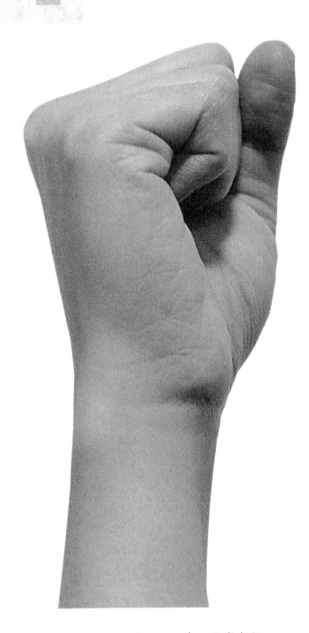

At first I was so happy that I didn't have to draw fingers!

Tracing the outline seemed simple enough!

There was barely any negative space to note!

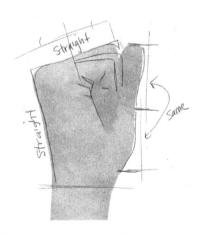

Relationships and lines looked very straightforward.

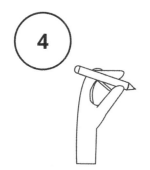

4 The outline on this one takes a bit of effort, but then again, don't they all? The depth and difficulty in this hand position lies in the fact that it's all created with equal amounts precise drawing and careful shading. Take your time and refine carefully.

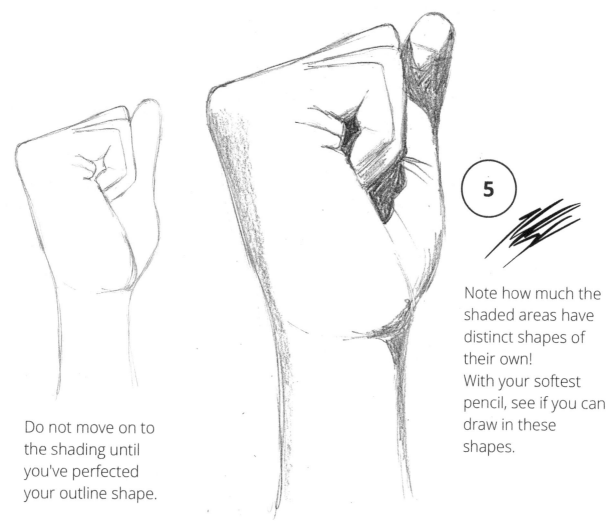

Do not move on to the shading until you've perfected your outline shape.

5

Note how much the shaded areas have distinct shapes of their own!
With your softest pencil, see if you can draw in these shapes.

The other tricky thing about hands and shading is that there are often different values (shades of grey) within the shadows. This means you have to work on creating the correct gradations from black to white, on each separate area within the hand that is shaded (which, is a lot most of the time)!

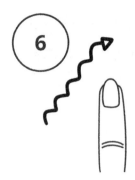

6 Pour yourself a cup of coffee and settle in for a serious shading session here. Carefully move from one area of the hand to the next, taking careful note of the shaded shapes, their gradations, and how the shading regions fade into the other areas of the hand. Try your best to recreate what you see from your photo in your drawing.

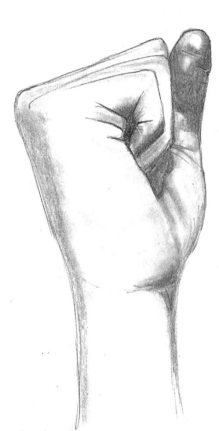

As always, use small bits of black pencil to punch up the contrast in the deepest parts of your shadows!

See the difference that small bit of black makes between the two drawings?

Scan every inch of your reference with your eyes and try to carefully record each wrinkle you see!

Make sure they are drawn in in the right direction!

Continue to use the side of your blending stump to move larger areas of graphite from a dark region to a light one. Use the tip of the blending stump to accentuate the heavier lines and wrinkles you see!

Make it Snappy

The subtle contrast of the fingers against one another and the fact that all five fingers have a mind of their own, make this one a challenge! Not to worry! The step-by-step approach will have you drawing this successfully in no time! Follow me!

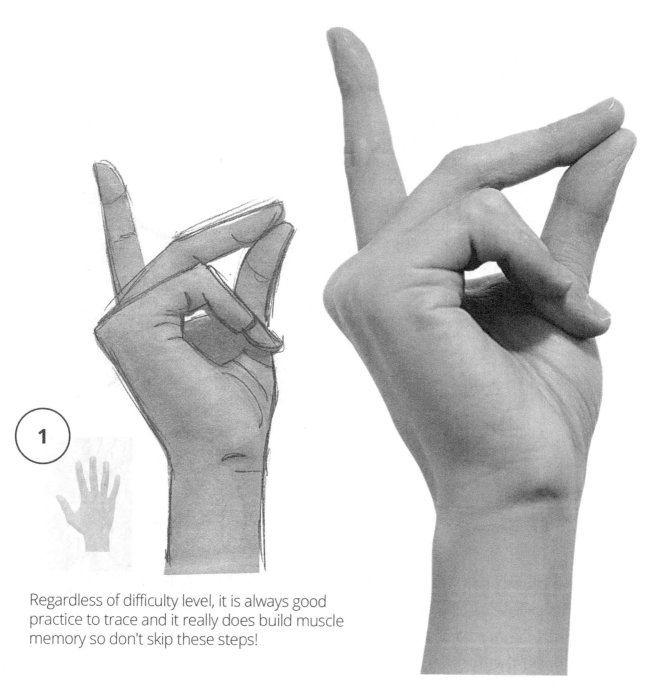

Regardless of difficulty level, it is always good practice to trace and it really does build muscle memory so don't skip these steps!

The negative spaces in this hand photo are super interesting! Taking the time to notice those shapes and angles at this stage really helped come construction time!

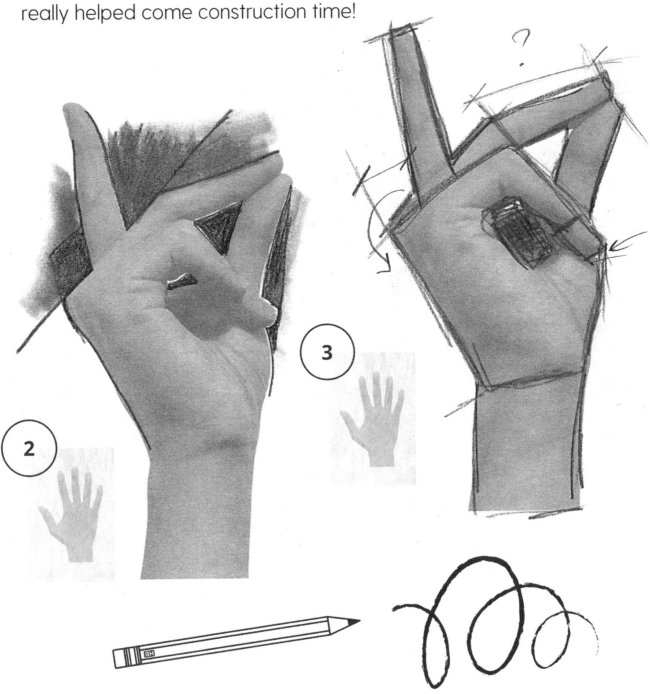

Seeing how all the angles and shapes and lengths relate BEFORE you put pencil to paper really gives you an edge on creating a successful drawing. That being said, this one (for me) proved to be a really big challenge; I'll be the first to admit it!

4 Start this one out very, very slowly. Feel free to check each and every line as you draw them (against your tracings) to make sure you're on track. It's better to check your progress frequently rather than winding up going too far down the wrong path (or finger)!

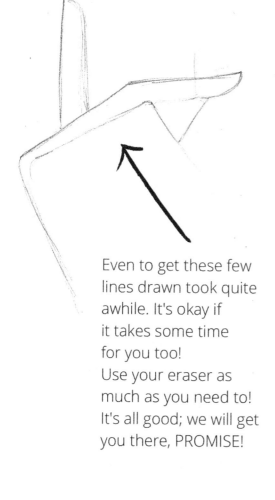

Even to get these few lines drawn took quite awhile. It's okay if it takes some time for you too! Use your eraser as much as you need to! It's all good; we will get you there, PROMISE!

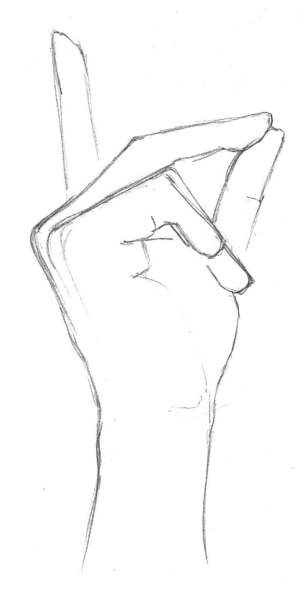

Slowly but surely, take your time to draw in all five fingers and that meaty palm. Do not give up! This is the hardest part! Once you get in the outline, you can relax and begin the shading.

5 Before you go onto the shading part, it's a good idea to go slowly over each and every part of the hand and finger with your eyes. Look back and forth between the reference and drawing. If you miss a bump here or a bit of tapering there, now's the time to fix it.

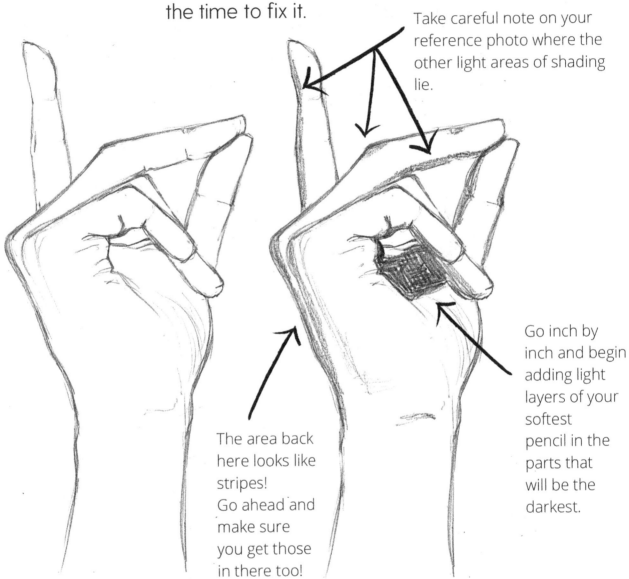

Take careful note on your reference photo where the other light areas of shading lie.

The area back here looks like stripes! Go ahead and make sure you get those in there too!

Go inch by inch and begin adding light layers of your softest pencil in the parts that will be the darkest.

Ignoring most inner details and shading, fingernails and JUST focusing on ONE aspect of the drawing at a time, will ultimately ensure your success! Only after the outline is 100% complete, consider adding the first bits of shading.

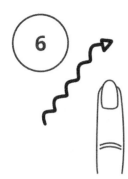

6 Shading is comprised of 50% pencil work and 50% blending tool afterwards. You can't do one without the other and they end up doing a little dance together as they take turns drawing and blending around each of the fingers and funky grooves that appear around each corner of the hand.

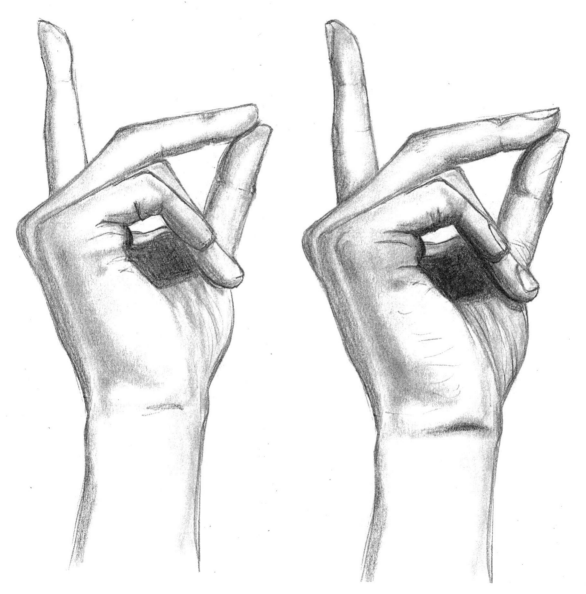

If you get lost trying to figure out how light or dark something is, just remember to refer back to your original photo reference! If you look closely enough, you'll find all the answers you are looking for!

The Hitchhiker

The thumbs up signal is a universal symbol for "good" so it is an absolute must in this collection of hand drawings! It's a nice reprieve from all those tricky fingers too! Let's dive in!

In the olden days, you could use it to catch a ride too!

As always, use the simple 6 step process laid out on page 17!

1

The blockiness of the fist is so different than what we would normally draw with hands. Block out anything that helps you think of this in a new or easy way to understand!

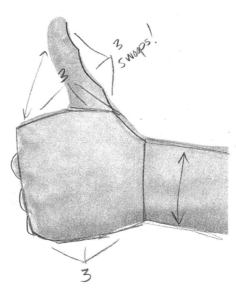

2

Note those fun little pockets of negative spaces.

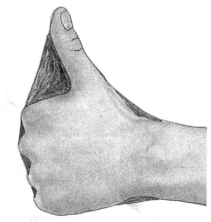

3

I find noting angles to be very helpful, especially as we are just about to draw!

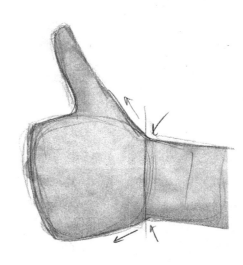

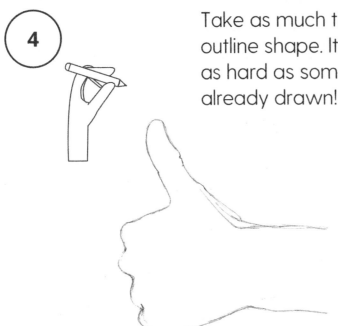

4 Take as much time as you need to build the outline shape. It's not easy, but it's also not as hard as some of the ones you have already drawn!

keep up the great work!

5  The shading on this one is super light. The easiest way to get very light shading is to be very gentle when you lay down graphite.

As always, use the side of your pencil for this step and then let the blending stump do the heavy lifting, which is in this case will be not heavy at all!

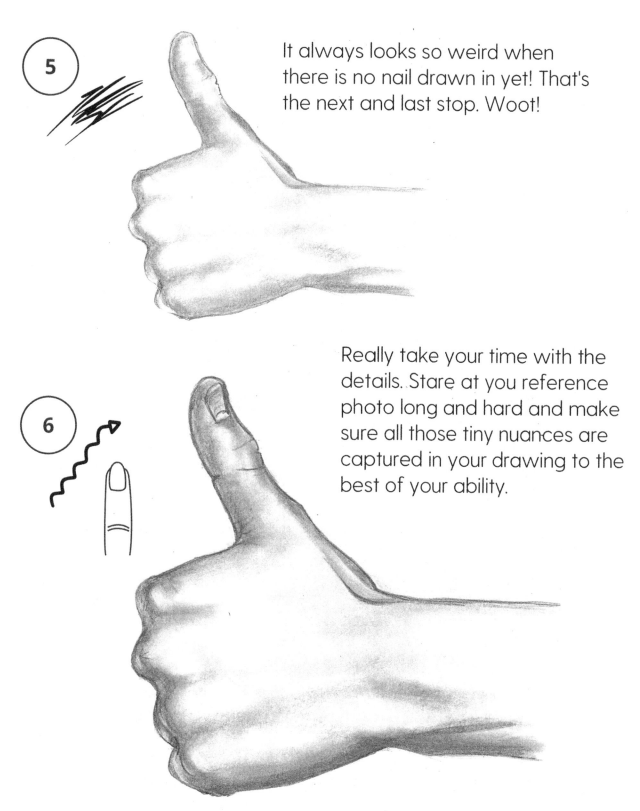

5

It always looks so weird when there is no nail drawn in yet! That's the next and last stop. Woot!

6

Really take your time with the details. Stare at you reference photo long and hard and make sure all those tiny nuances are captured in your drawing to the best of your ability.

There is a lot of intricacies in the knuckles so do NOT rush this final step. The final result and how well this "reads" as a thumbs up, all depends on the subtle shading and minute details that you put in in Step 6!

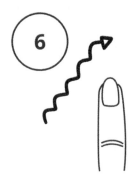

6 The best way to get accurate drawings is to keep comparing yours to the original photo reference that you have. Are the shadows in the same place? Are the highlights more or less okay?

Even looking at these side by side right here, it is obvious that I can add more shading on the thumb. See how my thumb is lighter than the photo? I should go back and darken the base of the thumb a bit more until it is dark like the picture.

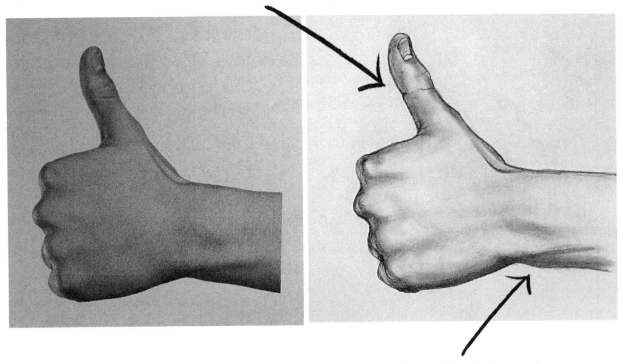

This little extra bump out doesn't exist on the original either. Oh well. Just take notice of these after you're all done and then you can go back and tweak the little details as much as you like!

It is SUPER helpful to wait a day or two and then go back and compare with fresh eyes. When I take a break, all of those minor mistakes just suddenly seem to jump out at me! Then correcting them is a cinch because they are so obvious.

Don't nit-pick too much though! Be happy you made it this far!! These drawings are such a big challenge and YOU'RE DOING GREAT!

 # Grasping at Straws

I love this one! It is elegant and only four fingers instead of five so it's just a tad bit less tricky.

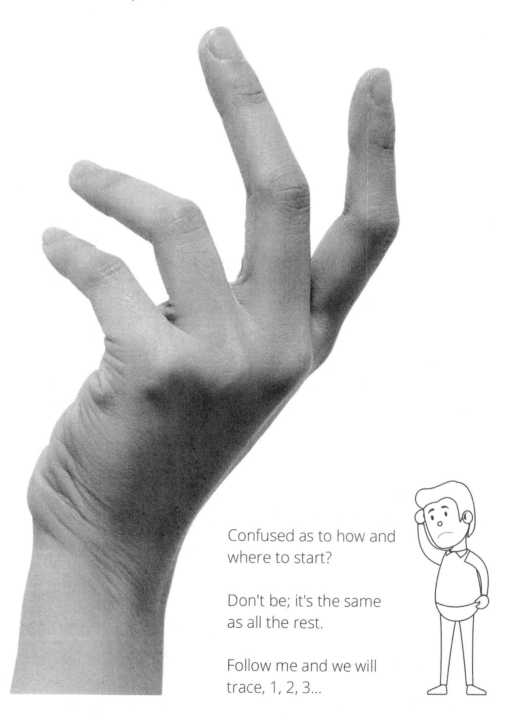

Confused as to how and where to start?

Don't be; it's the same as all the rest.

Follow me and we will trace, 1, 2, 3...

After drawing and tracing so many hands, it should be getting easier to draw those familiar moves that we see over and over again. Like the rounded tips of the fingers, or the thickness of the wrists.

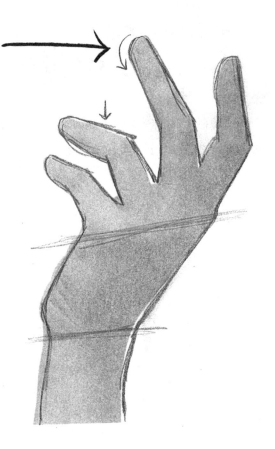

1

Still very much working on it!

Really analyzing these angles for this particular gesture is EXTREMELY helpful when it comes to actually drawing it. These relationships are everything! The practice of drawing the fingers and the close analysis of how they all sit in relation to one another is what will makes your drawing accurate!

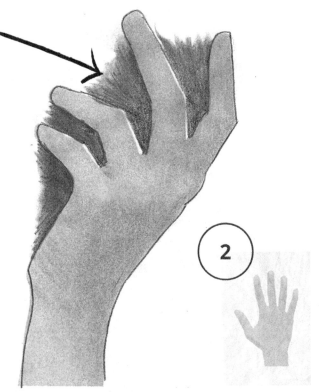

2

Too hard? Use the directions on page 18 to transfer the outline onto your paper.

3 My third trace is always the most informative. Little details and nuances start to jump out at me that I don't notice when I'm looking at the negative spaces around the fingers or the overall tracing practice for muscle memory. Also it gets to me look at other people's hands in real life with new eyes...

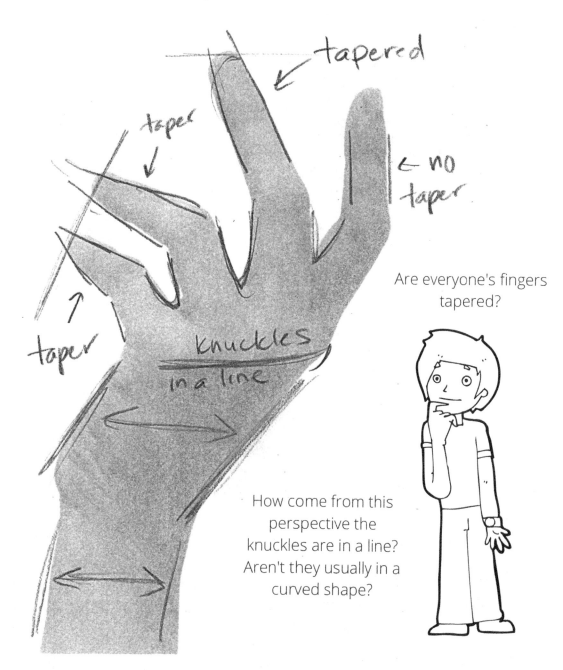

tapered

taper

← no taper

taper

knuckles in a line

Are everyone's fingers tapered?

How come from this perspective the knuckles are in a line? Aren't they usually in a curved shape?

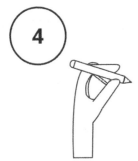

4 Drawing takes practice. Hand drawings take more practice than normal! You can see how far off my original drawing was.

That's okay! Use your tracings to help you see how on or off track you are and then make any necessary adjustments.

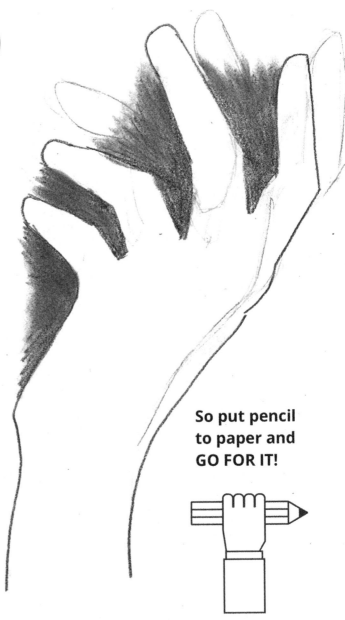

Bad! I know! But every practice is good practice and, over time, all those practices really count and make you awesome at drawing so KEEP IT UP!

And remember:

No one gets worse from practicing more; THAT'S NOT A THING!

So put pencil to paper and GO FOR IT!

4 Sometimes it can take a long time just to get to this point; that's okay! Be patient and make those adjustments, little by little, until you finally have the basic outline all finished.

After collecting information, analyzing the shapes and practicing your drawings on trace, it is time to draw! Start with just the outline.

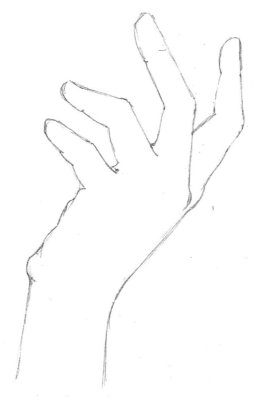

5

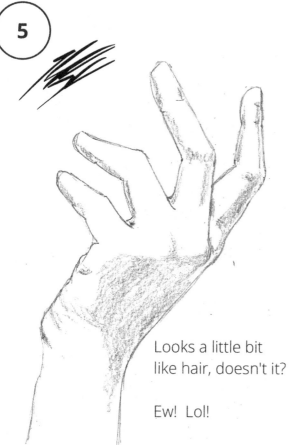

Looks a little bit like hair, doesn't it?

Ew! Lol!

The cool part is that shading is next, and that's when things get easier and you don't have to be so exacting. Just begin by laying down a little bit of graphite where you see the areas are darkest on your reference.

5 To get the best dimension and improve how your hand will "read" from afar, make sure to make use of your entire value scale. That means using all the greys from white and black and everything in between. To do this effectively, it is often necessary to do two or more passes of graphite over the darkest areas.

This hand has one layer of graphite spread around pretty evenly.

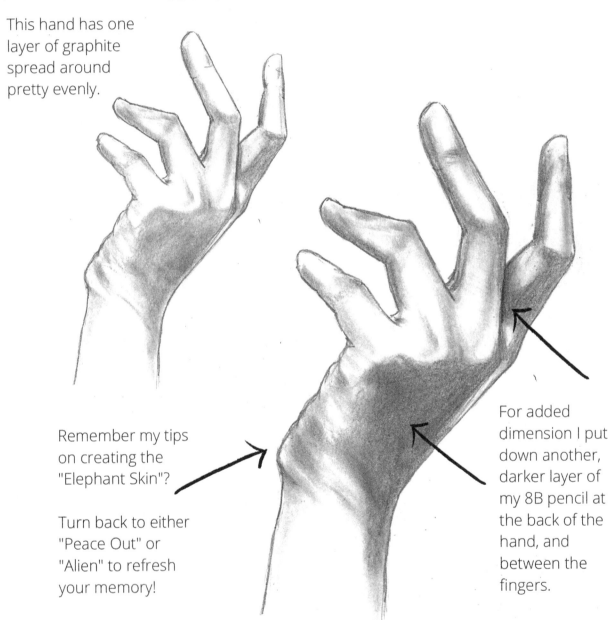

Remember my tips on creating the "Elephant Skin"?

Turn back to either "Peace Out" or "Alien" to refresh your memory!

For added dimension I put down another, darker layer of my 8B pencil at the back of the hand, and between the fingers.

94

At long last the hand is done. Make sure you navigate with both your eyes and your pencil, around every tiny millimenter of your drawing to make sure you haven't missed any teeny tiny detail, wrinkle, fold, highlight or fingernail!

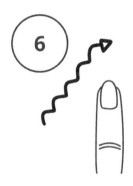

Don't forget that your eraser is a powerful tool in itself!

You can carve highlights, accentuate knuckles and clean up your edges.

Pretty awesome!

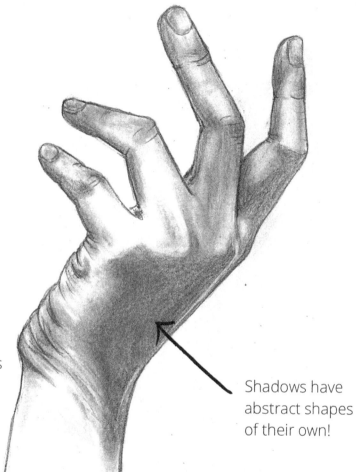

Shadows have abstract shapes of their own!

Show your artwork off to friends and family...and fur babies! I bet they will be so impressed!

Although Tippie looks more impressed with herself than with my drawing! Lol!

The Lover

I couldn't make a whole book on hands and not included the universal symbol for love. I also loved drawing this one and hope that you do too.

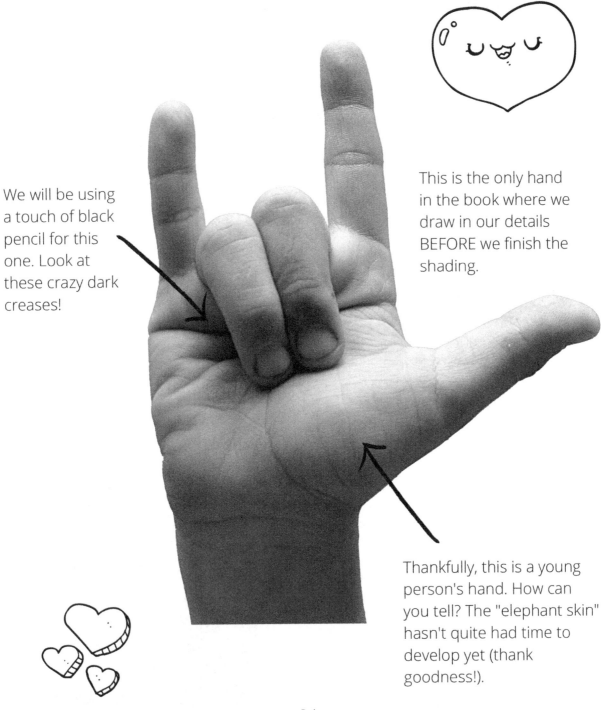

We will be using a touch of black pencil for this one. Look at these crazy dark creases!

This is the only hand in the book where we draw in our details BEFORE we finish the shading.

Thankfully, this is a young person's hand. How can you tell? The "elephant skin" hasn't quite had time to develop yet (thank goodness!).

If you are short on time, you may skip the muscle memory building part of the tracings. Instead, just do an overall outline. Then use the outline as a ruler against which you can use to compare your subsequent attempts. I think you will find this so incredibly helpful!

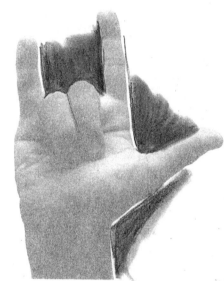

Again, you can see all of those negative shape triangles. The top shape came in particularly handy this time (omg, see what I just did there?).

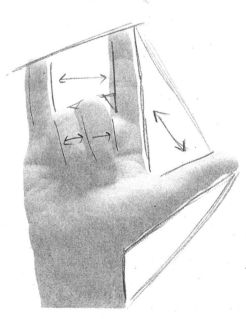

More parallel lines and triangles to note. Breaking down the confusion of the hand into basic shapes and parts and lines really helps to demystify what is truly going on! At least that is the hope!

It's important to take a stab at drawing each hand gesture, even if you're not feeling confident. It is truly the only way to become better at drawing. Just use your tracings to guide you and help you, but don't use them as a crutch or you won't improve!

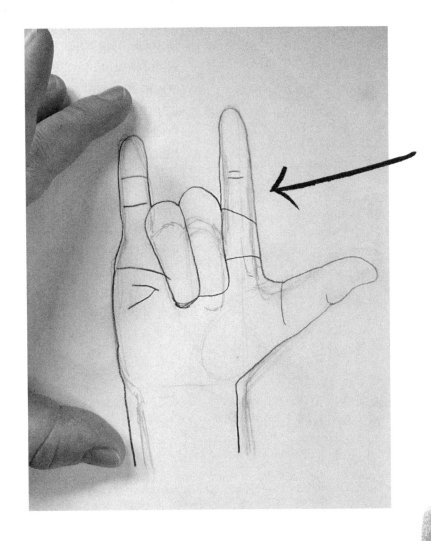

My overall shape was pretty good!

My middle (bent) fingers were terribly off.

I should have referred to my negative shape trace to help me more! I would have certainly drawn that part better had I taken more time to use that as a guide.

Next time!

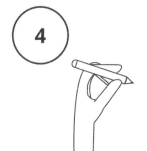

4 Take your time to make those corrections and then finalize your outline.

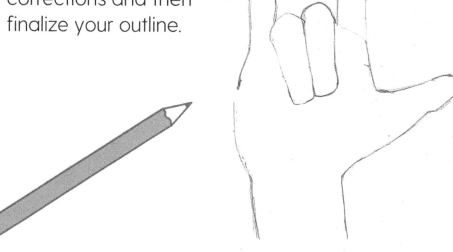

5 Using the side of your softest pencil, lay down graphite into these areas. If you're not sure where to start adding the graphite, refer back to your original reference!

5 While looking at the photo reference, it becomes strongly evident that the shadows on this hand are directly due to the creases within it.

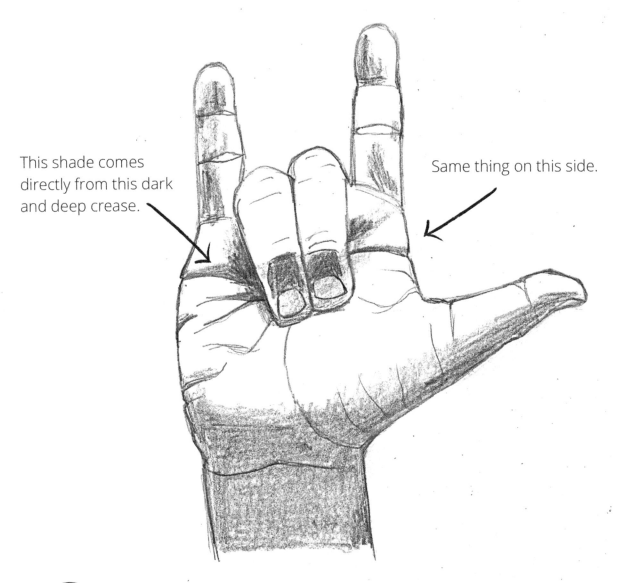

This shade comes directly from this dark and deep crease.

Same thing on this side.

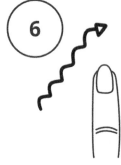

6 Normally I wouldn't add the details until the very last step but in this case I had to add them in before I even started to blend the graphite in. That way you can get much more accurate shading done, and in less time, with fewer corrections.

5

So then after the details (Step 6) we will return to shading (Step 5) to finish. As always, directionality is super important! To get the most realistic and accurate shading, remember to hold the blending stick in specific ways to help you get the results you want.

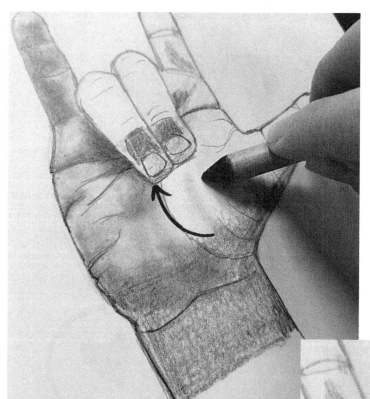

Using the side of your dirty blending stick, sweep the stump in curved, broad strokes. This mimics the shape of the palm and spreads the graphite evenly and smoothly, in the same direction as the creases on the hand.

When you need to accentuate a super dark crease, like the ones on this palm, use only the tip of your blending stump and really grind in that graphite. This time the aim isn't to spread the graphite, but rather to deepen the look of the crease.

Using only graphite, add second and third coats to darken and deepen the shadows in the darkest shadowy areas.

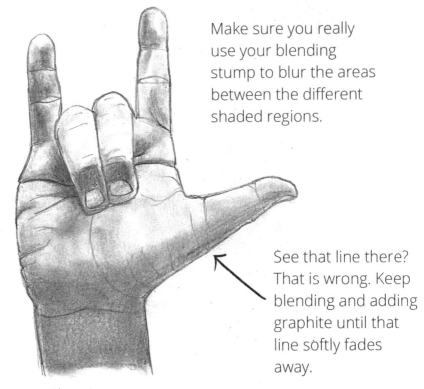

You should never really see a line where you've added darker areas, but rather it should appear like a very smooth gradation from dark to light.

Make sure you really use your blending stump to blur the areas between the different shaded regions.

See that line there? That is wrong. Keep blending and adding graphite until that line softly fades away.

Add touches of black in the deepest recesses of the palm and creases for a highly realistic effect!

YOU DID IT!!

The Loser

I just love this hand gesture (the sign language symbol for "L") and the hand model too! The lines of this hand are so angular and sharp, it almost has a cartoon look about it!

Get your tracing paper out and let's get started!

We will start right at the beginning of the 6 step process to begin! It worked for the others so far, I know it'll work for this one too.

1 As usual, the first tracing can be used for both muscle memory building as well as a measuring stick to see how you're doing when you get to the drawing stage (step 4).

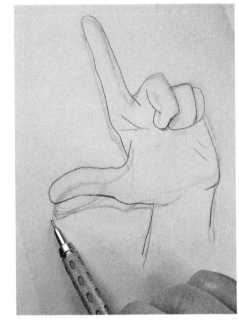

Not too shabby!

2

Here we have that collection of triangles we see! This time, five!

I now can't look at a hand and not think of this!

3 I LOVE the swoops and swishes of the angles in this photograph! Makes the drawing so dynamic and fun to try and reproduce! See you in step 4!

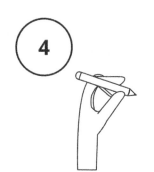

4 Drawing this one was is challenge, but a fun one, thanks to the angular lines and definitive swoops! Use your tracings to help speed up the process!

As you practice drawing more and more hands, you will become faster and faster at drawing them. Your observational skills will also slowly start to improve and you will start to see the hand and fingers as a mere collection of shapes, curves and lines, and not as a "hand". Before you know it, this will all be easy!

5

There is a lot of shading in this one! Start by laying down an area of dark graphite in the middle of the palm under the fingers, along the wrist and lower palm, and along one side of the forefinger.

Get your blending stump ready, we have a lot of graphite mooshing to do!

5  You can get a lot of shading done relatively quickly, just by holding your blending stump this way.

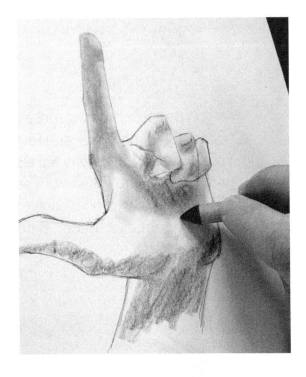

5  You will almost always need at least two, if not three or four layers of graphite to get the right amount of shading (and therefore depth) to your drawing. Don't rush it, just layer it up so it looks awesome!

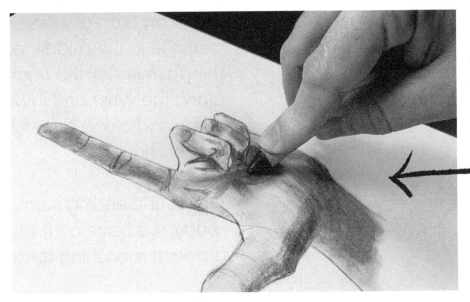

Holding my stump like this gives me a ton of extra power to drive the graphite into the areas that I want!

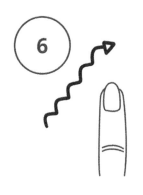

6

You may find that you have to do a lot of pouncing (gentle bouncing) with your large eraser to lift out areas that you've shaded too aggressively. That is perfectly normal.

If it helps you to put in the wrinkles and weird bits sooner, go for it!

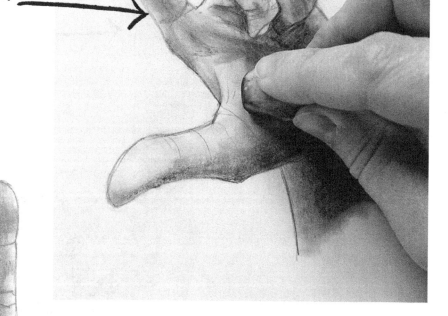

6

You may just have to put them back in if they get blended out.

That's okay too.

This stage of the game can look rather messy.

Remember though, shading is 50% pencil work and 50% blending and that's why this looks half done. As soon as you take the time to blend, everything will all fall beautifully into place.

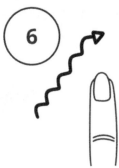

6 I really had fun with this one and I hope that you did too! Take your time and carve out any highlights that you might have missed. Add in black pencil to the inner, black core of the shadow areas, and take your time sketching in those wrinkles and palm lines too!

Make sure to add this little bump out here; it's where the joint separates the top part of the finger into two places.

Fingers always remind me of worms with all of their segments!

Please tell me that's not just me!!

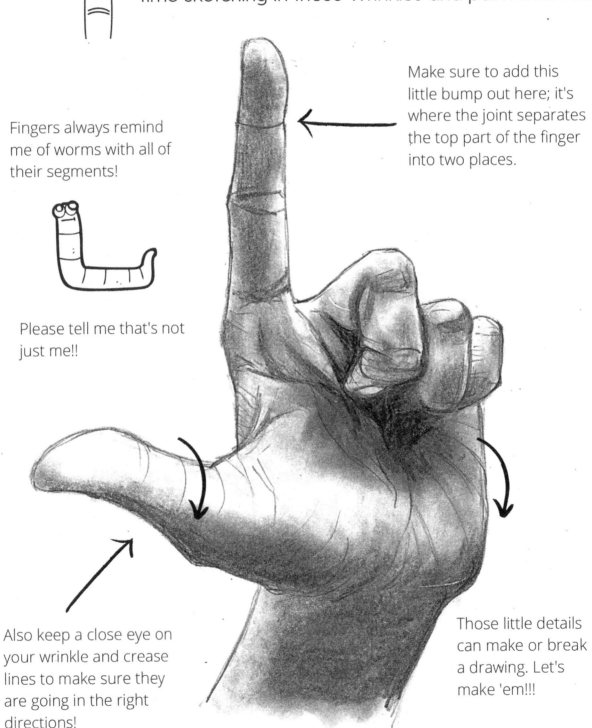

Also keep a close eye on your wrinkle and crease lines to make sure they are going in the right directions!

Those little details can make or break a drawing. Let's make 'em!!!

This is a handy hand position to know how to draw, don't you think? It universally means zero and is the letter "o" in sign language. It's also unique because it manages to hide fully two of the five digits! The shading patterns in this hand gesture are really cool and I did enjoy using my blending stump to create the shading patterns that I saw.

This hand gesture introduced me to a new hand feature. It's similar to the infamous "elephant skin" that graces the palm of practically every adult.

The squishy weirdness between the forefinger and thumb I am naming "Poodge," and it is equally daunting!

I wish I could say the drawing of this "Poodge" was easy, but, unfortunately for me, that wasn't the case at all! But thanks to my trusty tracings, I could manage to get the shapes down after while! Perseverance is key with these drawings! They are not easy! Use the 6 step method and follow me...

At first glance this shape seems super simple enough! You will be finished with your first trace in no time.

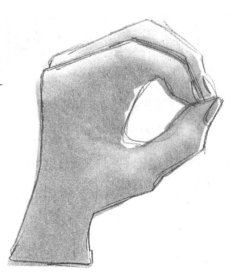

When you get to the negative space trace, watch out! There are 10 (yes TEN) bumps within this little circular area. T-E-N!

That's okay. The more you process these little details BEFORE you begin drawing them, the less of a shock it will be come drawing time!

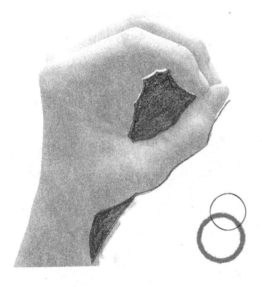

It is during the third trace that you may start to notice the strange "Poodge" area I was referencing on the Hand Anatomy page of the book...

Oh hands! Why must you always be so troublesome?

No worries, if you can learn to REALLY truly see the folds of the skin as just a series of shapes and shadows and highlights, you will be able to draw Poodge with the best of them!

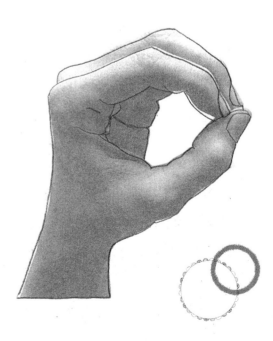

110

4

When faced with such a difficult gesture, I cannot stress enough the importance and usefulness of those first few tracings!

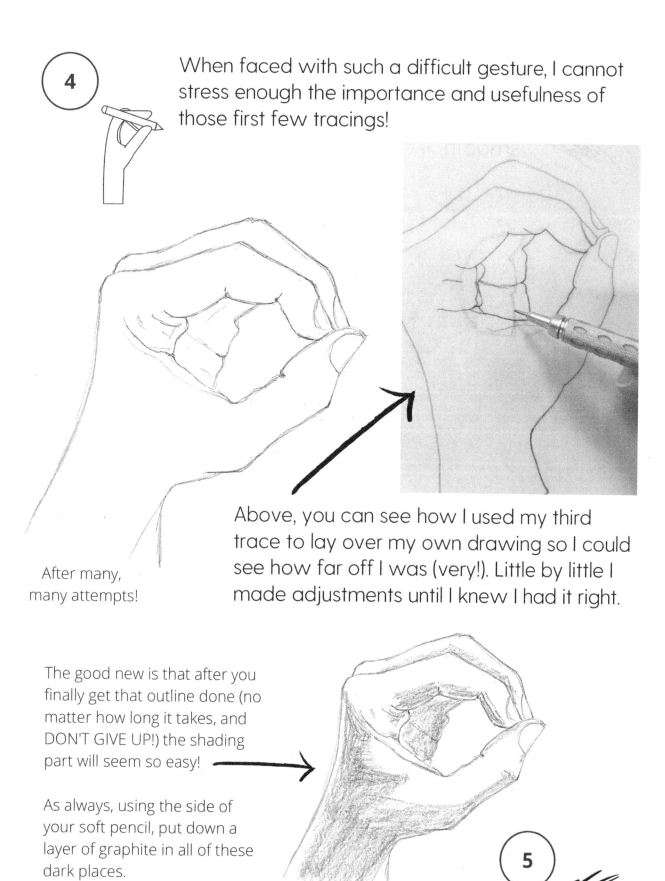

After many, many attempts!

Above, you can see how I used my third trace to lay over my own drawing so I could see how far off I was (very!). Little by little I made adjustments until I knew I had it right.

The good new is that after you finally get that outline done (no matter how long it takes, and DON'T GIVE UP!) the shading part will seem so easy!

As always, using the side of your soft pencil, put down a layer of graphite in all of these dark places.

5

5  Take your dirty blending tool and smoosh all of the graphite around until it's nice and smooth, like this!

Then begin putting down a much darker layer of graphite in the center of the "poodge" area!

To get a darker value, push down harder with your pencil. It's as simple as that!

There is a LOT happening in the complicated folds of the "Poodge"! Take your time to really analyze this section of your photo, so you best navigate that with both your pencil, and your eraser.

5 Thanks to technology, we can zoom in on these troublesome areas to get a closer look!

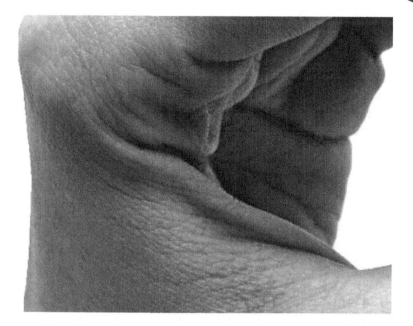

Yikes!!

That may actually be too close!!

Perhaps the "poodge" is better viewed from afar afterall!!

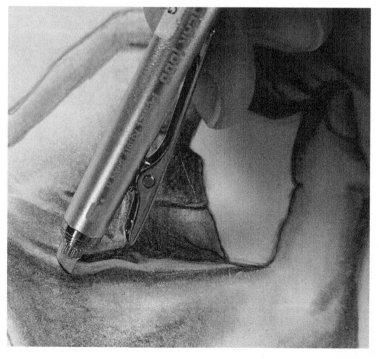

Pay attention to this photo! That erasing part is key!!.

I started by adding in the dark part of the shadows. And then, using my eraser from the back of my pencil, I "carved" out the light portion of the skin fold.

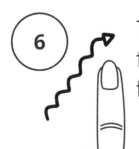

6 There may still be some careful sculpting that needs to be done in order to get the final outcome looking good!

This one is tricky but the overall effect is quite impressive if you follow through.

I truly hope that you do!

Still quite a bit more sculpting of the lighter areas with my pencil eraser.

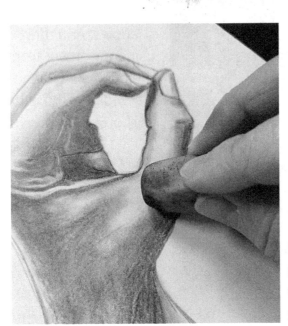

It also may be necessary to "pounce" away areas that contain too much shading. Pouncing will make sure that you don't get undesirable stripes of white in your shaded areas!

6 If you lose perspective it may be that you're working too long or too closely to your paper!

Take a few hours off and come back with fresh eyes, you'll be amazed at what you see!

Take note!

Poodge is lookin' pretty darn good actually!

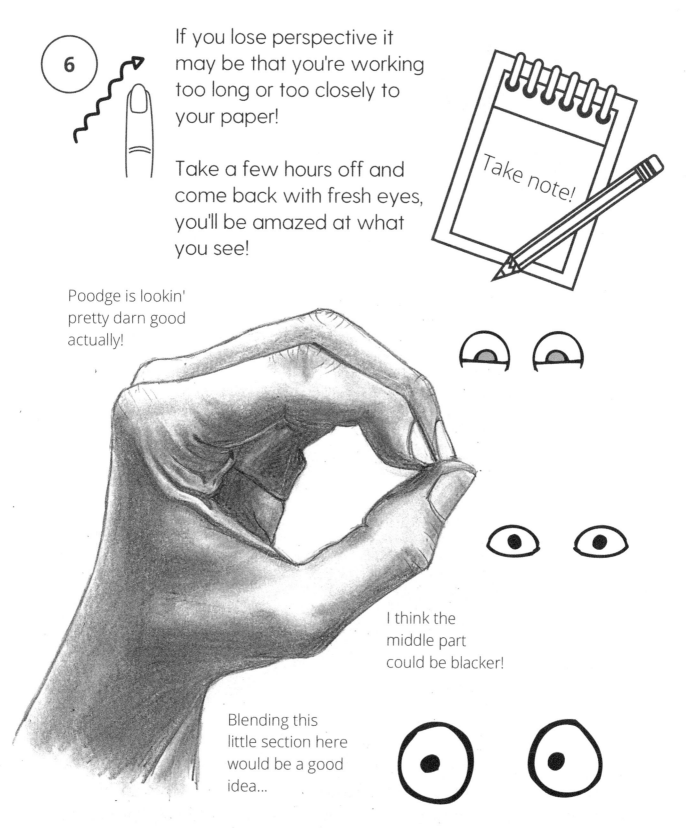

I think the middle part could be blacker!

Blending this little section here would be a good idea...

But at some point you need to call it a day! Be proud of yourself for attempting this one; it isn't easy!

Chunk

Is there anything cuter than a chubby baby?! No!! I simply couldn't resist putting this one in! Before we attempt a child's hand, I though it would especially fun and interesting to go all the way back to humble human beginnings, and try our hand at a big fat squishy baby! Why not?!

As soon as you start tracing you'll start to appreciate just how different a babies hand is from an adults. The good news? No "Elephant Skin!" Woo hoo! The bad news? This chunky monkey's hand is so completely UNlike an adults hand, it's like you're really starting from scratch! That's okay, the process stays exactly the same. Follow me!

1 As soon as I started the tracings I knew this one was going to be a challenge! While fingers on an adult are typically straight on the back (nail side) and slightly bumpy on the inside, babies' hands (at least extra healthy plump babies like this one) are nothing but a series of bumps and lumps. Oh boy!

ALL CURVES!

Do what you have to do to engrain these puffy shapes into your brain! Trace that little hand a hundred times if you need to. Relax and get the feel of all those curves!

Oh boy, can you imagine drawing a chubby little foot?!

2  This is the first time that the negative space trace may not do much to help my brain with the final drawing. Nonetheless, it will still help you understand and emotionally prepare for the drawing task ahead!

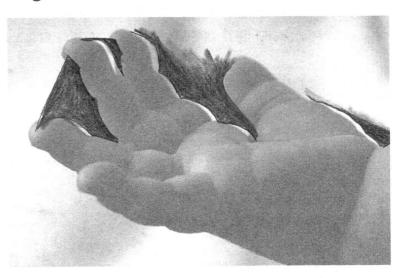

3  You'll get a little more information from the third trace. For example, you may pick up on the fact that where the little nails are, it's straight! It's also helpful to note the angles of the wrist and finger relations. Whatever else helps you, write it down.

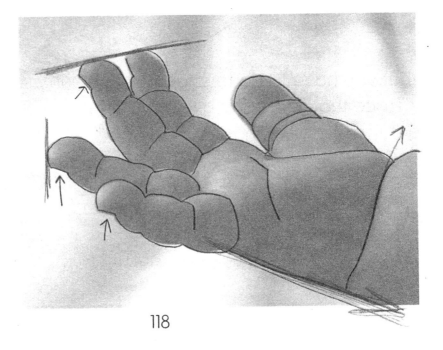

(4) Don't draw too much without checking on how you're doing. You may find (like me), you sketch the whole hand and THEN compare it to your tracings only to find out (too late) that you're way off! If that happens don't worry, that's what erasers are for!

Big time
way off!!

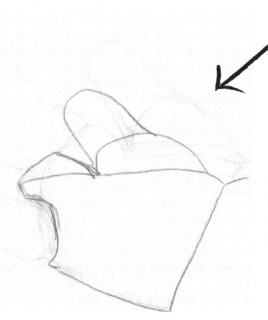

That's okay though. Little by little keep drawing and checking it against your traces until the final outline is drawn correctly.

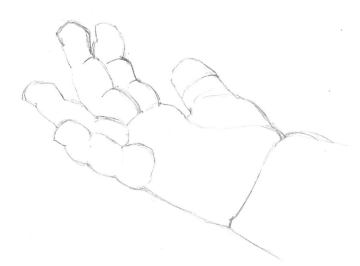

Just RELAX.

This isn't a race and these drawings are challenging! Take your time and get this outline part right. The farther down the drawing path you get, the harder and more work intensive it is to make corrections!

Chill out.
Take your time!

4

Now that the outline sketch is correctly drawn, take your time to perfect it. Add any details that you may have missed.

You can push down a little harder with your pencil once you've determined the final lines.

Really carefully, comb over the reference photo and add in the major lines!

5

Now we can finally begin the shading part! We will need to do 3 (or more) passes of graphite to complete the drawing. The first attempt should look something like this:

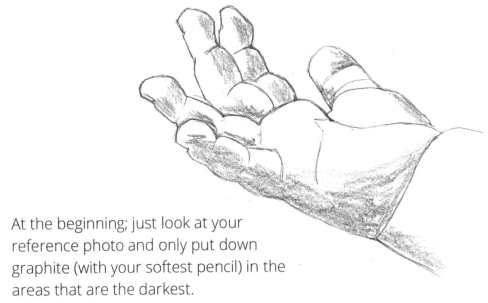

At the beginning; just look at your reference photo and only put down graphite (with your softest pencil) in the areas that are the darkest.

5 Don't rush this step. Put on some music, relax, and spend time laying down your graphite and blending it until it's completely smooth.

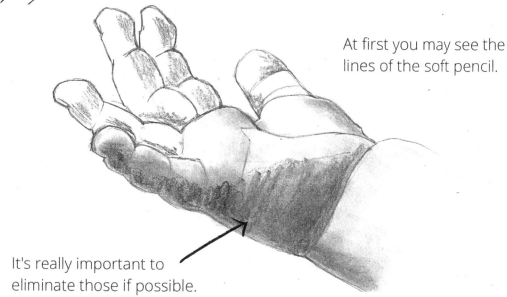

At first you may see the lines of the soft pencil.

It's really important to eliminate those if possible.

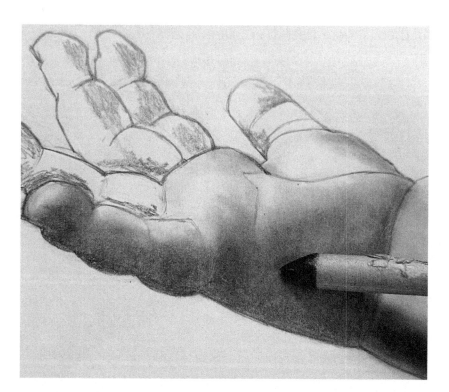

Just apply firm pressure, make sure your blending stump is nice and dirty, and keep mooshing around that graphite until all those lines are eliminated! You can do it!

121

5 Add a second layer of graphite to all of the darkest areas of the hand (which in this particular photo, is everywhere!).

Use your larger eraser to easily and quickly "pounce" away areas that need to be lighter!

Really stare at your photo reference and see: What areas are the lightest? What are the darkest? And then try your best to emulate that!

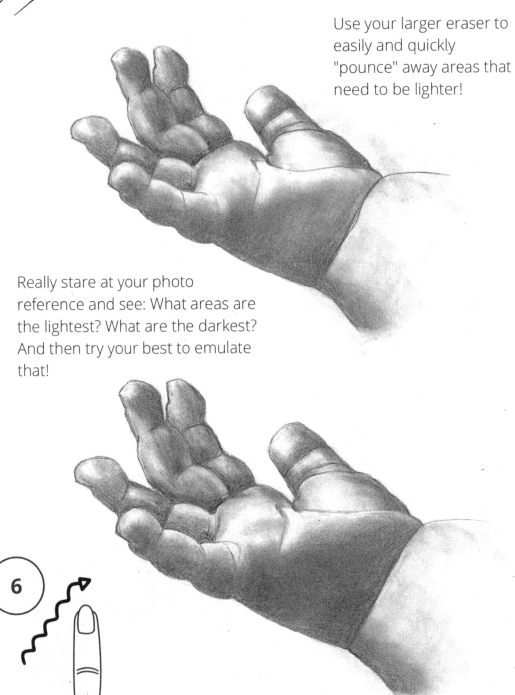

6

Fine tune and add more graphite until your final matches the photo, or as close as you can get!

Child's Prayer

I was excited to try a child's hand after the baby one, to see how it would compare. Good news! This set of smooth fingers is much much easier than those chunky baby fingers!

The best news of all?

NO "elephant skin"!!!

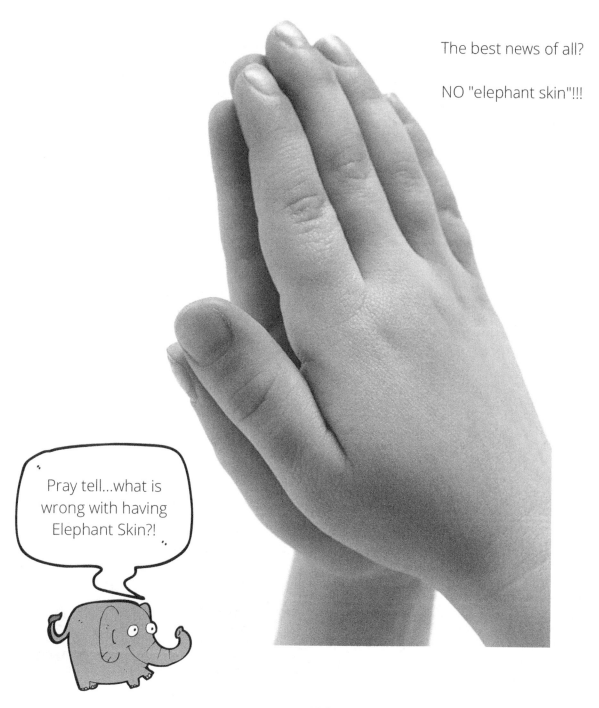

Pray tell...what is wrong with having Elephant Skin?!

1 As always, the first tracing is pretty straightforward, especially for this drawing. All the fingers are straight and even though there are 2 hands to draw, there are hardly even any details to worry about!

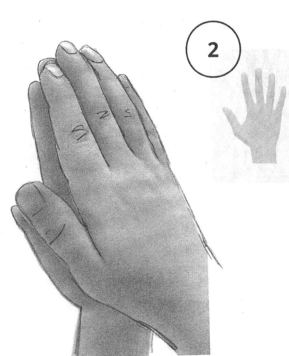

2

I think it's fascinating that all the negative spaces in this gesture are triangles. 8 of them!

3

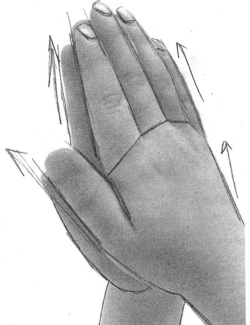

Really studying those angles is important and is also a huge help come drawing time!

124

4

Drawing the outline is next! Remember to use all of your tracings to help check your work as you go!

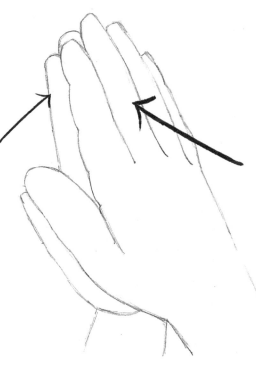

I drew the second hand last. That made it easy to put the fingers in the right place.

I drew the outer hands four fingers first, and then the thumb.

5

There is not a significant amount of shading in this one. That doesn't mean you shouldn't take the time to shade though!

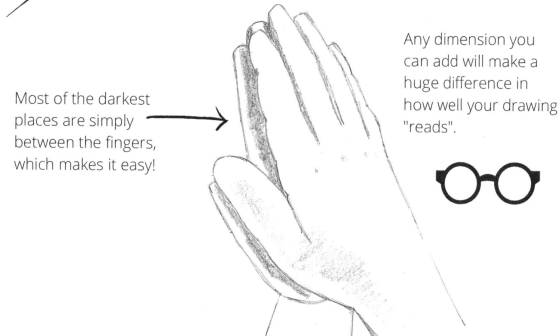

Most of the darkest places are simply between the fingers, which makes it easy!

Any dimension you can add will make a huge difference in how well your drawing "reads".

5 Keeping looking back at your reference to make sure you have enough shading in all the right places.

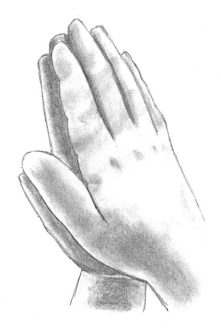

You will need to get out your black pencil to get these areas (between the fingers) to be as dark as they really are in the photo!

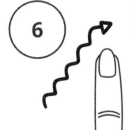

6 Carefully add the finger nails and knuckle wrinkles and you're good to go!

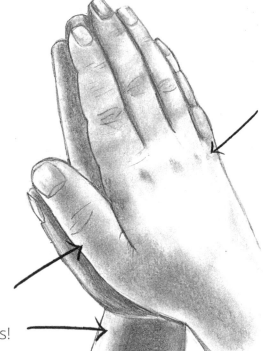

Use the very tip of your dirty blending stump to create these super subtle marks on the back of the hand.

I think I really love drawing children's hands!

Don't lose sight of those small but important highlights!

2 Hands, 1 Heart

Who doesn't love a heart-shape hand sign?! It's so perfectly wonderful every single time! This one may look daunting but because there are so few veins, bones and wrinkles, it's actually pretty straightforward!

Tracing this one makes me especially happy. Look at that heart! Both this and the negative space exercise really help me to understand what is important in this piece.

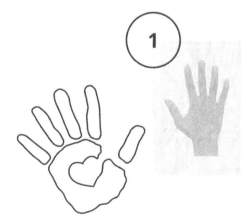

127

2

This top triangle is very helpful when it comes to drawing the final piece.. Hold this piece of trace paper drawing over the sketch and see how far off (or how spot on) you are! Then make the changes accordingly!

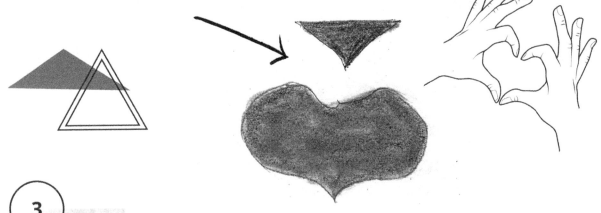

3

Again, angles, angles, angles...are so important! If those angles are off, your whole drawing will be off. So take the time to note them here and then recreate them as best you can on your own paper.

4 Take your time with the drawing outline portion. Those angles are tricky! Compare your lines against your traces and make the changes accordingly!

5 The hands shown in this reference photo are fairly dark. Whether that is due to the lighting or due to skin color, when trying to replicate shading in a graphite drawing, the reason is actually quite irrelevant! Our only task is to try to draw what we see. To get started here, simply apply graphite to the entire area.

Using the side of our soft pencil, of course!

5 The more involved the lights and shadows, the longer we will need to spend time on this step. That's okay; just relax and enjoy yourself! Take as many passes as you need to build up the darkest areas.

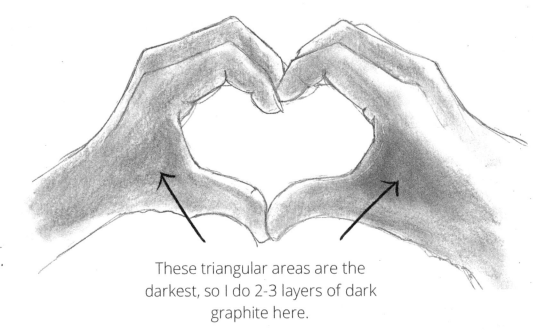

These triangular areas are the darkest, so I do 2-3 layers of dark graphite here.

5 You can "reserve" the highlighted areas by just leaving it the white of the paper OR you can shade it in and then erase out the shapes!

It's a win-win and totally your choice!

5 The little eraser on the back of my mechanical pencil is perfect for carving out the highlights in this drawing, especially along the thin, long, bones at the back of the hand.

Larger areas can easily be lightened by lightly going over them with a broader eraser.

Take too much off? Using your blending stump to add it right back! Easy peasy!

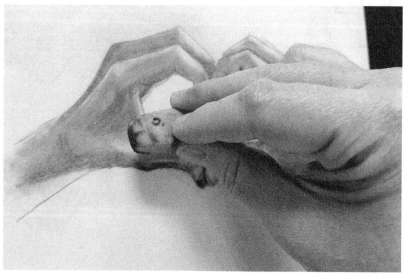

Sometimes you have to go back and forth between the eraser and blender. That's cool; don't sweat it!

5 Hands that are this intricately highlighted by the sun may take quite some time to get right. Just slowly comb over each finger and part of the hand until you think you have all the highlights and shadows properly recorded!

6

At long last! The details. Not much really, just a few wrinkles and nails and you're DONE! Great job!

Listen Up!

This hand gesture reminds me of when I was little and in trouble. My mom would get up in my face with her pointy forefinger, just like this and talk sternly to me and she always started with, "Listen up!" and then continued on with her lecture. Mom if you're reading this, (and you're my editor so I know that you are!) I love you and I'm sorry for all the horrible things I did when I was little!

Don't worry mom, I know (deep down) you love me!

The hardest part of drawing hands is trying to accurately capture the wonky angles of everything! Use your traces to really study the directionality of the fingers and their relationships to the rest of the hand parts so when it comes to drawing time, you are one step ahead.

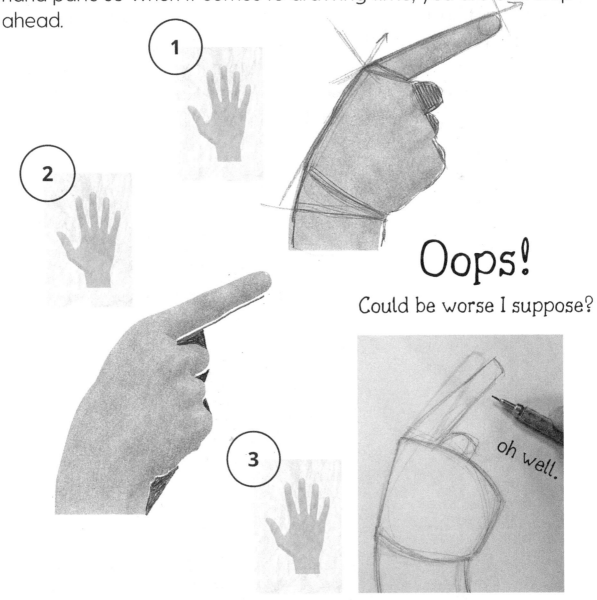

Oops!

Could be worse I suppose?

oh well.

That being said, you still may need to make corrections. Go easy on yourself! Drawing hands is hard. Just do the best you can and keep in mind that drawings done without the tracing pre-drawing exercises have a much larger chance of being totally wrong than if you hadn't taken the time to focus and study before you began.

Take all the time you need to do your tracings. When you're ready, go ahead and make your final outline. I think you'll find that the angle of the wrist and finger are the most difficult parts to get and that all the other odd bumps and lumps are not so difficult (at least I hope!).

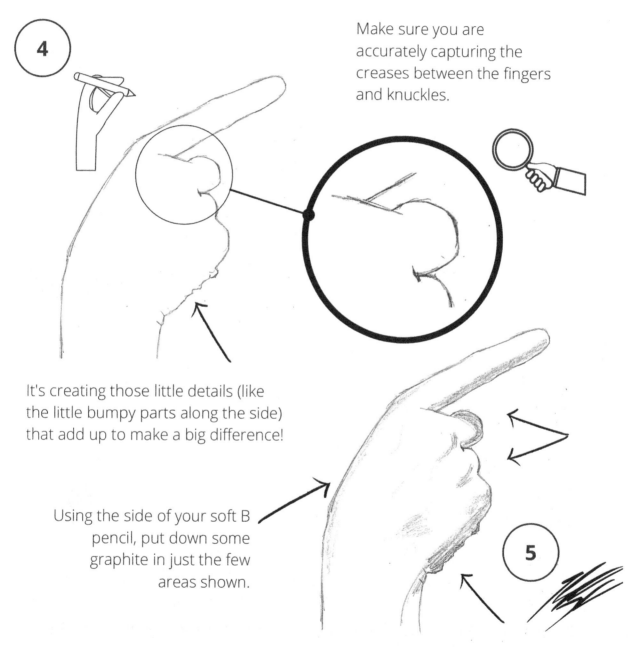

Make sure you are accurately capturing the creases between the fingers and knuckles.

It's creating those little details (like the little bumpy parts along the side) that add up to make a big difference!

Using the side of your soft B pencil, put down some graphite in just the few areas shown.

Shading in this hand is very subtle. Be careful not to put down too much. Remember to look back at your reference photo often!

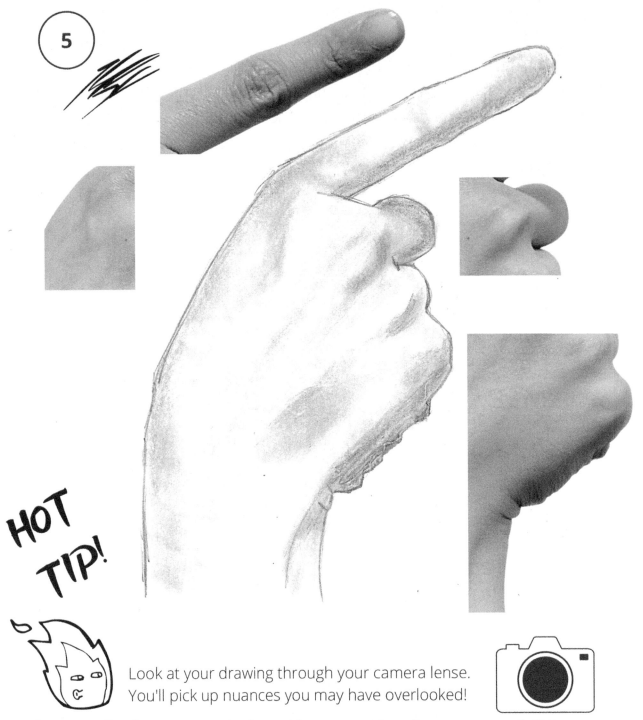

5

HOT TIP!

Look at your drawing through your camera lense. You'll pick up nuances you may have overlooked!

If you're feeling overwhelmed by your shading responsibilities, consider dealing with just one part at a time. Start, for example, with just the pointer finger. Just add the darkest part of shading where you see it in the photo. Then move to the middle knuckle. Then slowly, around to the different parts of the hand. Seeing it in pieces, rather than the whole, can make your job less daunting.

6

For a crisper look, more defined look, try creating a darker, bolder outline around the hand with a soft pencil.

Use a thinner mechanical pencil (like a .3 or .5) to create the thinner wrinkles and fingernails.

Leaving behind areas of white creates a strong contrast next to even light shading.

Use your eraser to "carve out" where the bones appear at the back of the hand.

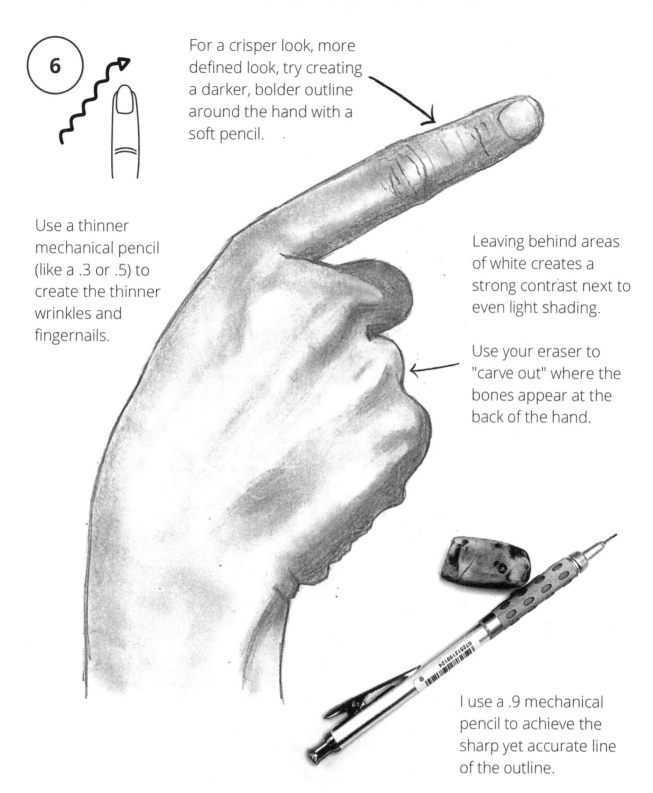

I use a .9 mechanical pencil to achieve the sharp yet accurate line of the outline.

I think sometimes smooth, wrinkle-less, back-side-of-hands can be just as tricky as Elephant Skin and Poodges! With smooth skin you have to deal with the subtle nuances of very slight knuckles bumps, perhaps just a hint of a tendon and only lit bit of shading to make it all look miraculously three dimensional! Good luck. WE GOT THIS.

Is there ANYTHING cuter than a sweet old Grandpappy with their cute Grandbaby? NO! Let's GO!

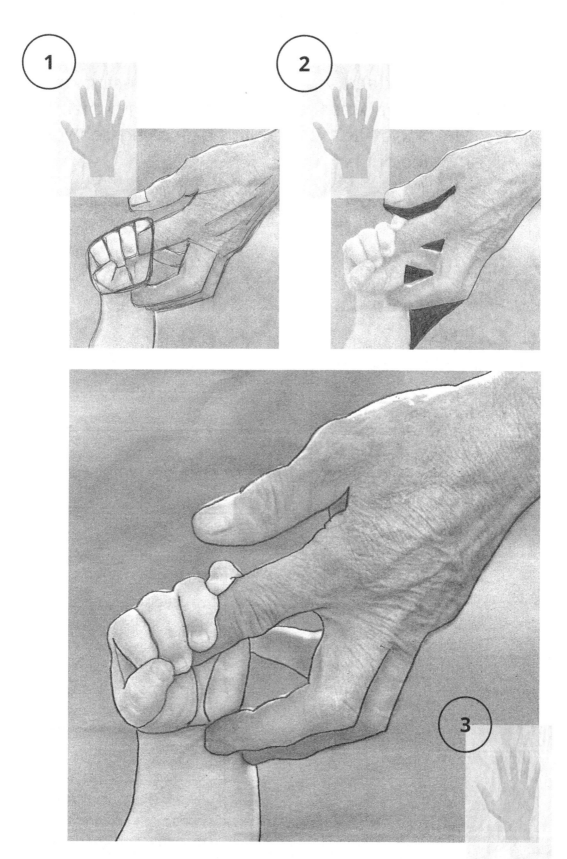

As always, trace to build muscle memory, note relationships and get emotionally prepared to create a very challenging picture!

4 It is perfectly normal to erase and restart a hundred times when approaching a subject as complex as this one. Start by looking back at your trace papers.

Begin your drawing with the overall shape of the baby's hand. Then block in the fingers.

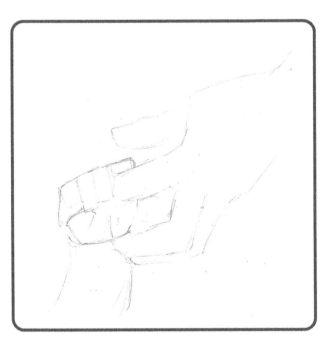

Once the baby's hand is in place, try to locate the forefinger of the man's hand. Do your best to block in the other fingers.

Use your negative space tracing to help you sort out the correct gaps between the fingers

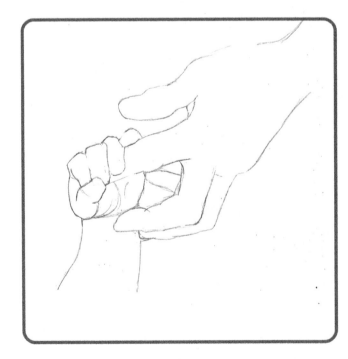

Take as much time as you need, to get all the fingers blocked out.

Then slowly but surely, use your observational skills to see every part of each hand as it truly is.

Working your way around the drawing with your mechanical pencil, start to adjust and tweak the hands, fingers, and spaces as they appear on your photo.

5 Start with the baby's hand and add some graphite to the areas that appear shaded in your reference photo. Blend well with your blending stump.

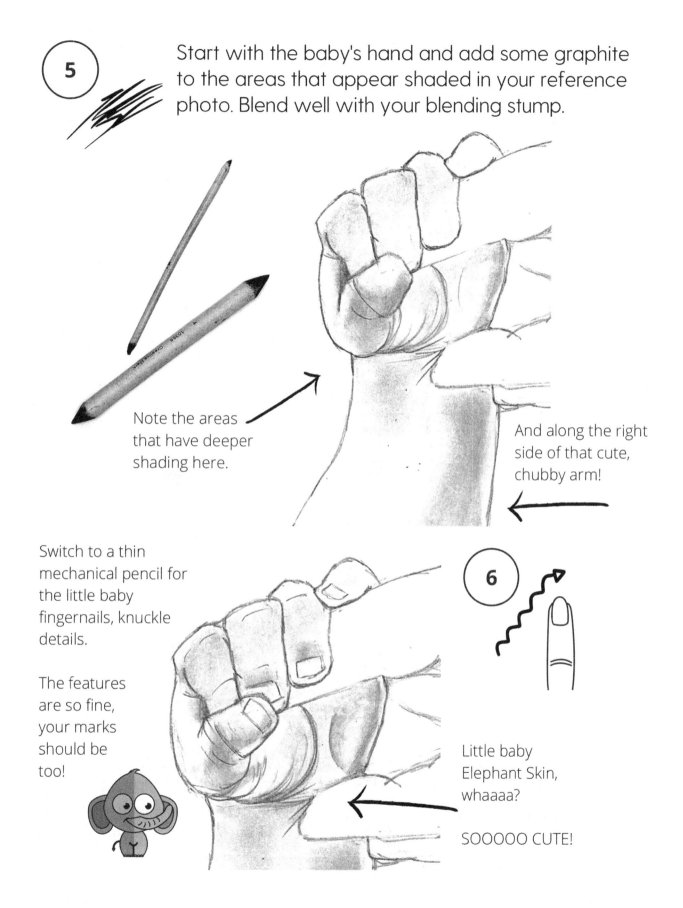

Note the areas that have deeper shading here.

And along the right side of that cute, chubby arm!

Switch to a thin mechanical pencil for the little baby fingernails, knuckle details.

The features are so fine, your marks should be too!

6

Little baby Elephant Skin, whaaaa?

SOOOOO CUTE!

5 Now it's Grandpa's turn! He has super dark skin (well, compared to baby's) so start with a nice overall shade of graphite to get started.

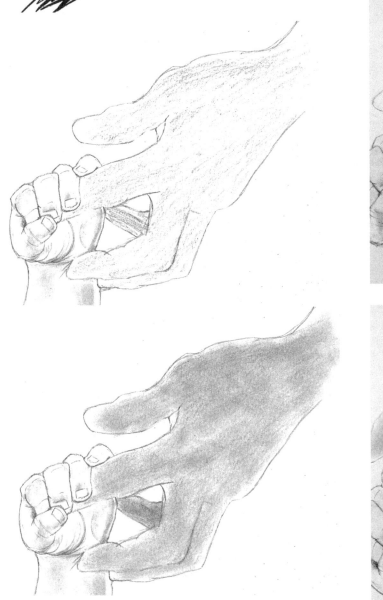

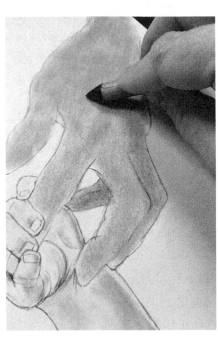

Let your tools do the hard work for you. Make sure you are using a really soft pencil (like 8B or 9B) and hold it until it is almost parallel to the paper! This allows you to shade an entire hand in the least amount of time. Do the same with your blending tool; the dirtier, the better!

5 There is A LOT going on with Grandpa's skin, so we are going to take this super slowly, one wrinkle at a time!

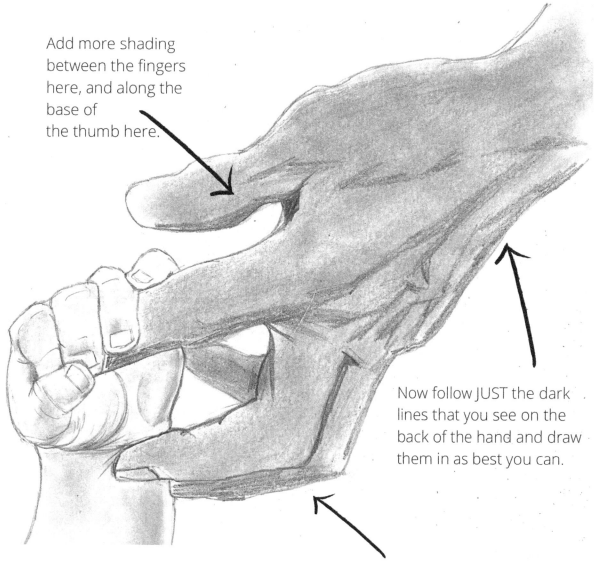

Add more shading between the fingers here, and along the base of the thumb here.

Now follow JUST the dark lines that you see on the back of the hand and draw them in as best you can.

Between the fingers and along the base of the index finger and this fourth finger here.

For this step, all I want you to do is add a little more graphite in the areas shown. Use your softest pencil and press down harder than you did before to make these areas darker. Refer to the reference photo to see if I am right! The dark areas actually have a little shape all their own, don't they? Can you see it if you squint your eyes?

143

5 Now comes the super fun part! With the back of your mechanical eraser (or any cool, small eraser), erase out lines along the pencil lines you drew in the last picture.

The white highlights appear due to the positioning of the lightsource (which I'm presuming to be the sun in this case).

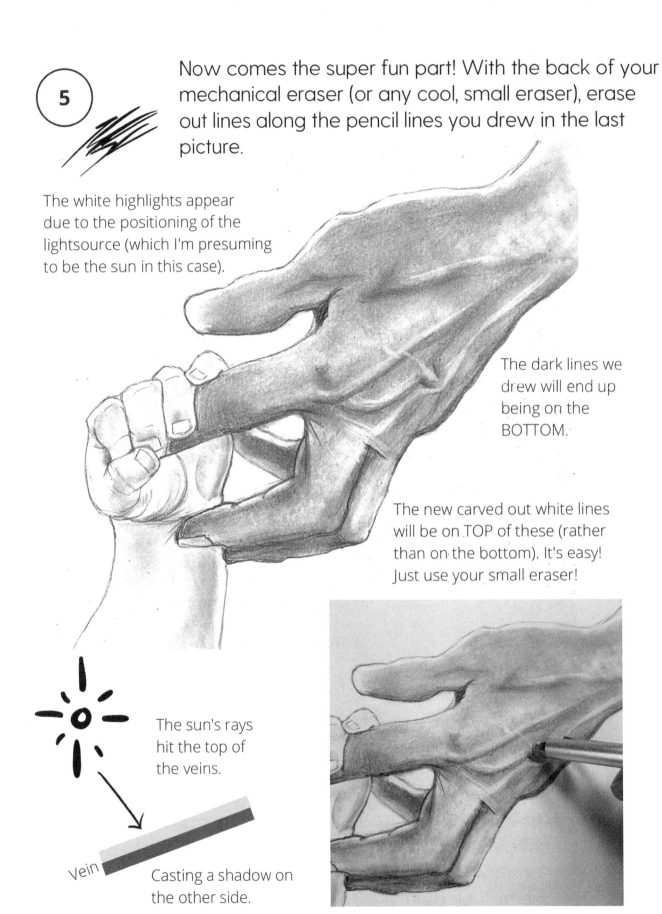

The dark lines we drew will end up being on the BOTTOM.

The new carved out white lines will be on TOP of these (rather than on the bottom). It's easy! Just use your small eraser!

The sun's rays hit the top of the veins.

Vein

Casting a shadow on the other side.

5 Now that all the highlights are carved out and all the shadows have been caste, it's wrinkle-drawing time! Use a wider lead (like .7 or .9) for the deeper creases and a thinner lead (like a .3 or .5) for the finer wrinkles.

Now is the time to take razor focus on every square millimeter of the sweet, old man's hand!

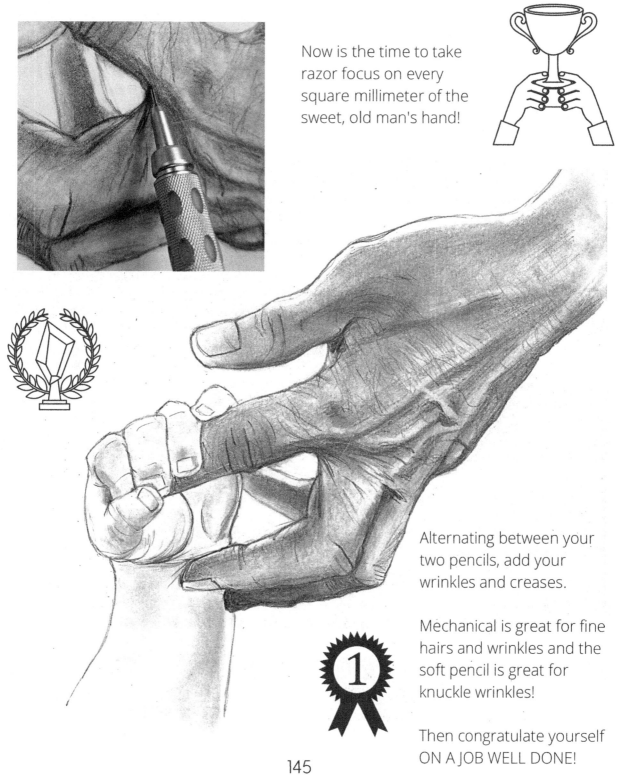

Alternating between your two pencils, add your wrinkles and creases.

Mechanical is great for fine hairs and wrinkles and the soft pencil is great for knuckle wrinkles!

Then congratulate yourself ON A JOB WELL DONE!

The Diva!

I simply had to included a pair of hands that featured a freshly manicured set of nails or this book would not feel satisfactorily complete!

No weird finger bends, no wrinkles, no Elephant Skin or Poodges to speak of, how hard could it be to draw these? Hahahahaha...VERY!

Thankfully, if you follow the 6 step system we have been following to draw all the hands in this book, you stand a fair chance of doing AWESOME(ly)! Let's get started!

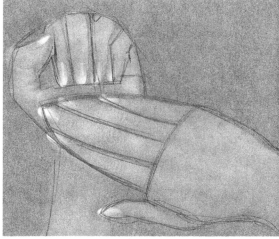

Grouping the hands into larger sections like this will definitely help you wrap your head around the shapes you'll be needing to start off with.

DO NOT SKIP THIS STEP.

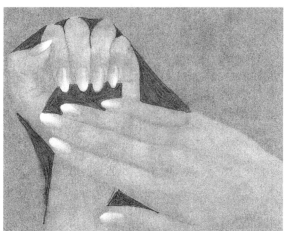

The negative space analysis may be a bit too complicated to be of much use for this pair of hands.

That doesn't mean it isn't helpful to stop and take note of everything while you color these regions in.

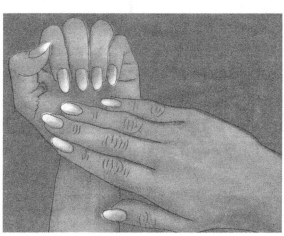

Straight-up tracing is always a great way to build muscle memory. Even if it doesn't help, it is guaranteed not to hurt. So do it.

4 Without further ado, it is drawing time.

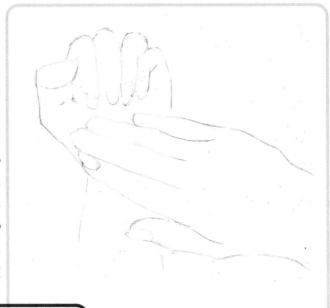

Start off slow and sketchy. Erase and redraw as many times as you need to. Use your third trace to double check your lines, every few moves, to make sure you haven't gone too far off track!

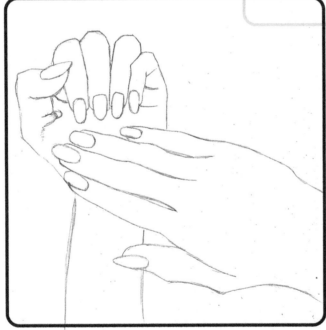

Once you feel you have the overall shapes correct, it is fine-tuning time.

Get out the original reference photo and study every inch of it. Compare it to your drawing as you make your way slowly around the hand, tweaking and refining as you go!

If you just can't get the outline (this nearly killed me!) do NOT feel bad if you resort to tracing. All the magic happens with the shading and the most important part ISN'T that you feel frustrated, it's that you feel great and are ready to power ahead to the next step. So someway, somehow, meet me at Step 5 and feel great about how you got there, it's all good!

5 First, as always, lay down a layer of graphite using the side of your soft pencil. This time though, because the skin color of this model is so fair, we can't just scrub graphite everywhere. Instead, we need to be judicious in our graphite application.

And although this isn't a man's hand, and it has no wrinkles, the back of this hand is not unlike the wrinkled Grandpappy a few pages back and we will approach it in the same exact way.

The drawings are treated similarly because veins and tendons are drawn pretty much the same way. The sun shines down on them, there's a light side and a dark side. It's as simple as that! Now let's take a closer look and break it down step by step.

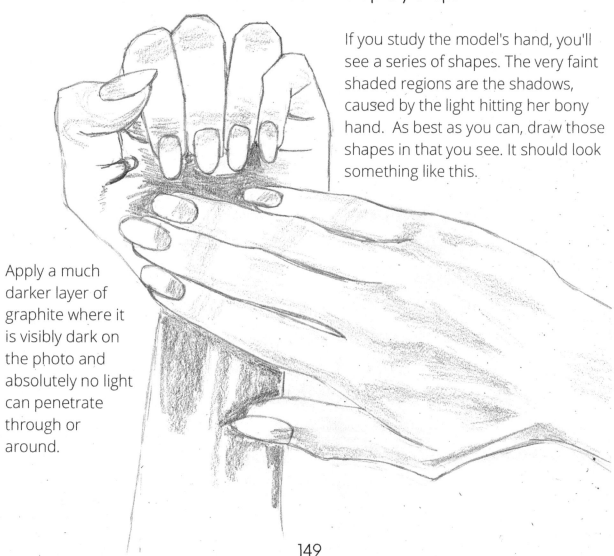

If you study the model's hand, you'll see a series of shapes. The very faint shaded regions are the shadows, caused by the light hitting her bony hand. As best as you can, draw those shapes in that you see. It should look something like this.

Apply a much darker layer of graphite where it is visibly dark on the photo and absolutely no light can penetrate through or around.

149

5

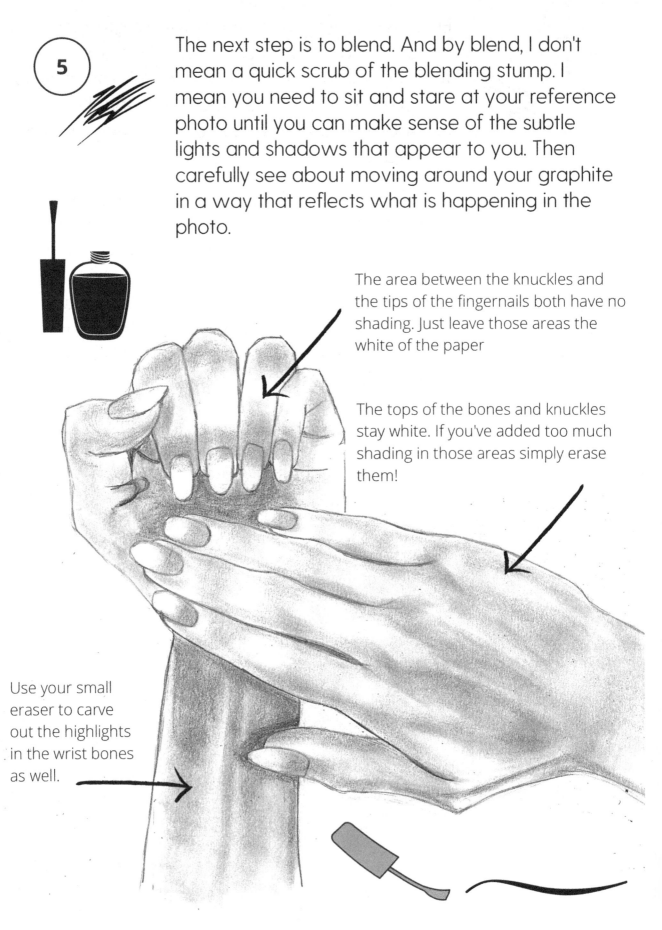

The next step is to blend. And by blend, I don't mean a quick scrub of the blending stump. I mean you need to sit and stare at your reference photo until you can make sense of the subtle lights and shadows that appear to you. Then carefully see about moving around your graphite in a way that reflects what is happening in the photo.

The area between the knuckles and the tips of the fingernails both have no shading. Just leave those areas the white of the paper

The tops of the bones and knuckles stay white. If you've added too much shading in those areas simply erase them!

Use your small eraser to carve out the highlights in the wrist bones as well.

150

The details on these hands are super fun! You'll need to make a highlight on each of the fingernails, but in order to do so, you first need to lightly blend graphite from the base of each nail to the tips. The base should still remain darkest, so if you have to go back and add more graphite at the base of the nails, go for it. The end result is so cool!

6

Once the nails are all slightly shaded, take your mechanical pencil back-end eraser and carve out a distinct highlight on each nail. From base to tip! Look at that shine!

Just swipe up!

First, with a fine mechanical pencil, carefully add lines to all the knuckles.

Use your soft pencil to make sure the Poodge crease here is good and dark.

Ooh la la!

Pinky Promise

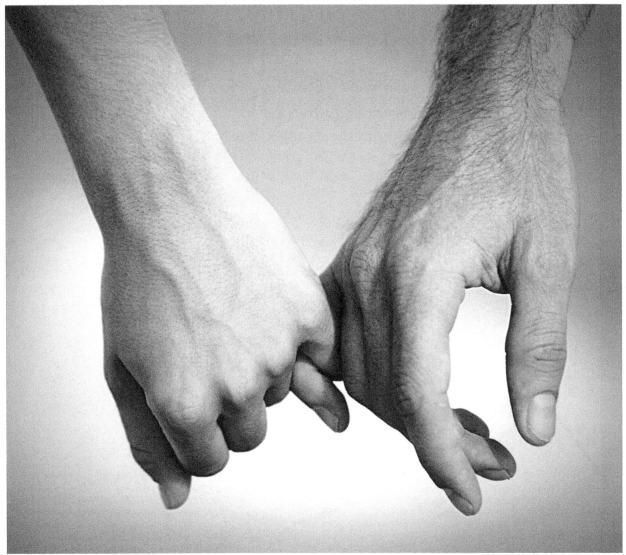

Last but certainly not least, the timeless pinky promise. An interesting, intricate hand holding gesture with hair, veins and wrinkles being the cherries on top!

Or something...

The most important factor to focus on when you're learning to draw hands is really your observational skill, not your drawing skill.

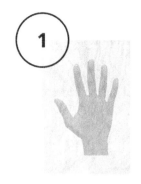

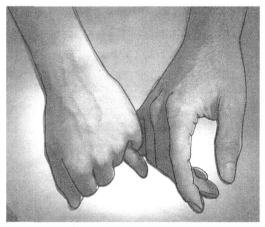

Straight up tracing will help your eyes and hand communicate better. You start to tune into details, shapes and relationships much better than if you just started to draw.

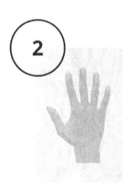

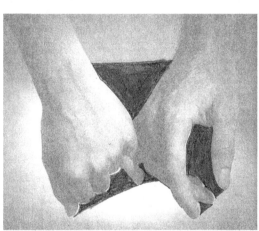

The top triangular shape is really helpful when trying to position the hands onto your own paper.

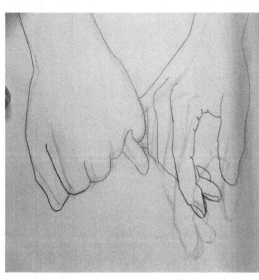

I wanted to show you how off my own drawing was after I took a stab at free drawing. Although my man hand is grossly oversized, notice what I got right: all of the negative spaces! Thank you trace 2! I'll take what I can get, and so should you. Then try again. That practice is how we learn!

When you learn to really, truly see things is when you really, truly start to become a better artist. Practice and patience is what will take you there!

153

4  Take as many tracings and as much time as you need to get an accurate outline. Hands are hard!! So don't beat yourself up if you don't get this your first time. I didn't either! The important thing is that you keep at it and don't give up.

Hey! Don't leave me hangin!

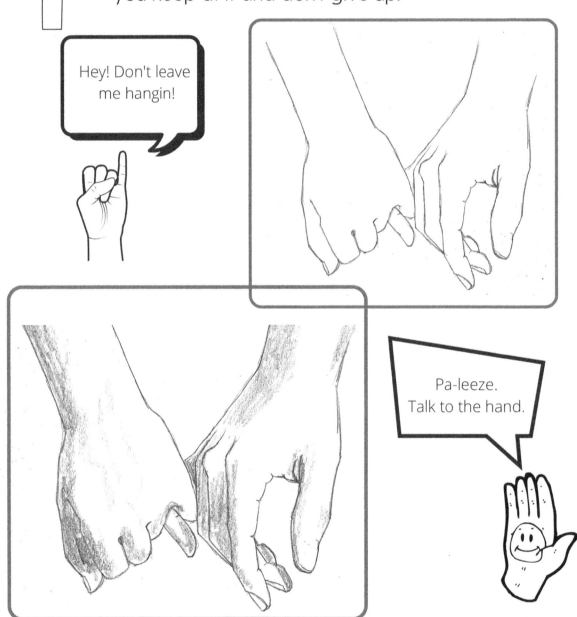

Pa-leeze. Talk to the hand.

5 Once you're happy with your outline, take a look back at your reference photo. Notice which areas are shaded and, using the side of your soft pencil, add graphite to those areas.

5 At this point, all there is left to do is the shading. Sounds simple, but hands that have veins and tendons need a lot of attention so that those subtle details show up accurately. I will lead you step by step through the shading process so you can clearly see all the little intricacies and nuances you can create using your trusty blending tool.

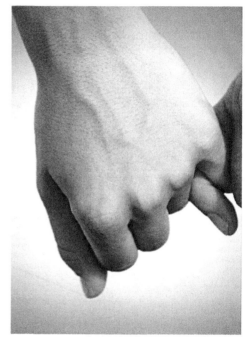

Always be looking back at your reference photo to see exactly which areas are light, and which should be darker. I am not inventing anything here, just trying to accurately record what I see.

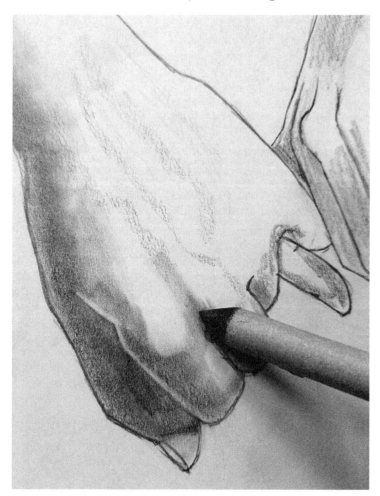

Areas that stick out the farthest are the lightest because the lightsource is hitting them first, casting a shadow off to one side. Here, the lightest areas are the knuckles and the tops of the veins. Those are the areas we want to avoid with our graphite. At this point, use the side of your blending tool to ease the graphite *between* all of the knuckles, careful to leave those highlighted areas untouched.

5 Now take a moment to look at the reference photo again. Notice how there is more than one shade of grey? For the medium and light grey areas, the one layer of graphite that you have already is enough.

Value Scale
in Pencil

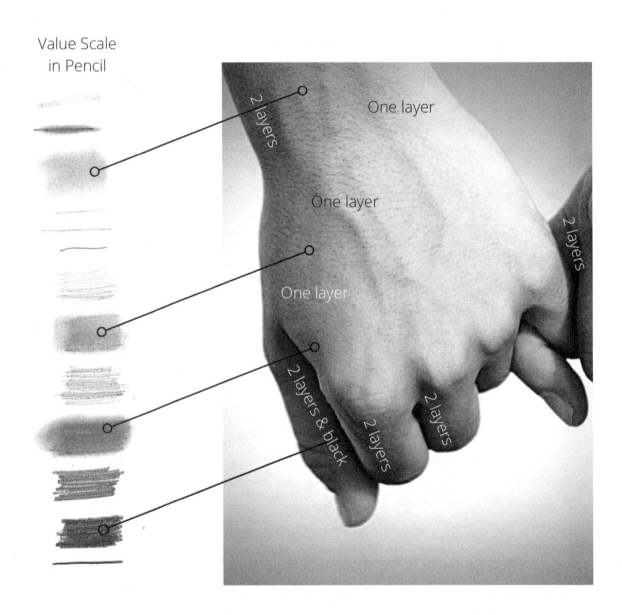

But for the darker areas, we will need darker shading. Add another layer of graphite in just those areas, pushing down on your soft pencil to get a much darker layer.

5 After you add the second layer of graphite it's time to be refining your shaded areas. Softly and slowly, start to draw the shapes of the knuckles. Add more pressure with your pencil in the regions we just discussed.

Notice the sliver of highlight along the forefinger. Carve that out with your small eraser if you've covered it with graphite.

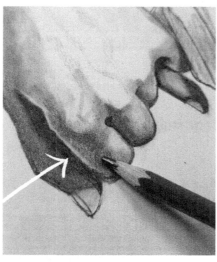

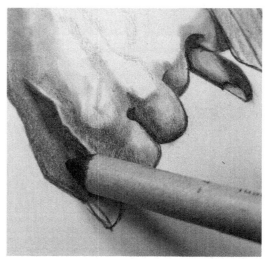

Veins or knuckles too pronounced? Add subtle shading using only your dirty blending stump without applying more graphite with your pencil.

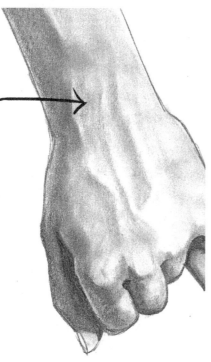

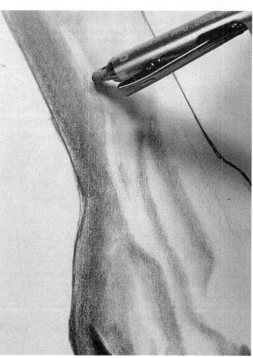

Use the graphite left over on your blending tool to lightly shade in the back of the hand. If the veins look like they are protruding too much, knock them back by shading them with your blending tool. If they aren't pronounced enough, carve out more white with your small eraser.

5 Now let's turn our attention to the second hand. Use the same blending techniques to render this one. With your blending tool, blend out the first layer of graphite. Leave the highlighted knuckles and bones lighter than the rest of the hand.

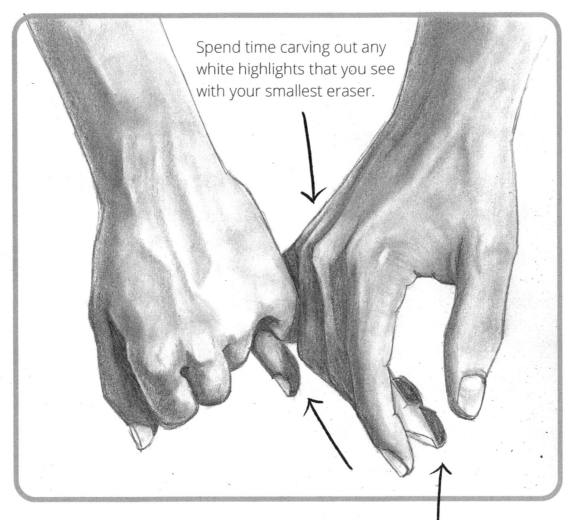

Spend time carving out any white highlights that you see with your smallest eraser.

Note that the shadows here are marked by a definitive line. That is very unusual, and fun to draw! Make sure not to overblend those areas so that the shadow line remains "crisp"..

Then add a second layer of graphite to the darker areas. Do not guess where the darker areas are, but refer to the reference photo. Here the darkest shaded regions are between the fingers and on the fingertips!

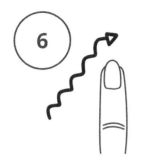

6 At long last! It's details time, and there are lots of them in this drawing! To be clear, you *must* make sure you are 100% finished with the vein and bone contouring first before moving on with the details in this drawing. Once you have the wrinkles and hair, you can't go back and fix any of the layers underneath.

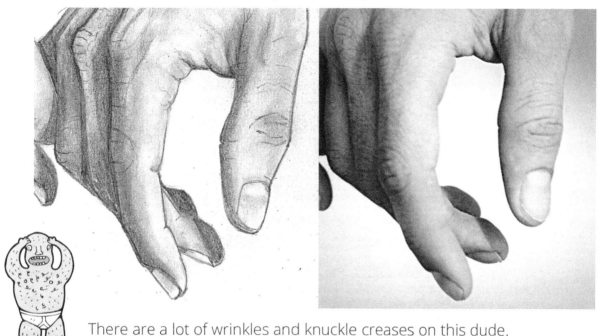

There are a lot of wrinkles and knuckle creases on this dude. Take your time and do your best to draw in what you see.

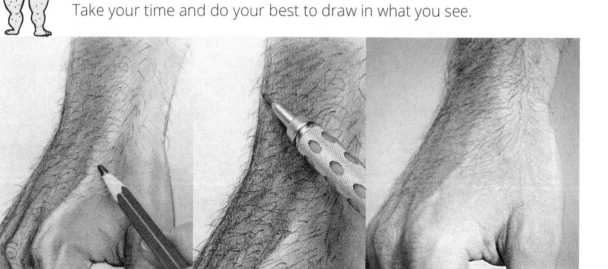

Let's all take a moment to be thankful we are only drawing this guy's hand...

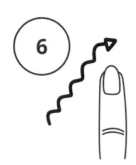

6

On close inspection, it became clear that there were two kinds of hair on this hand. A fine, downy layer, and a coarser, outer layer. It's also interesting to note that the hairs grow in different directions, depending upon where they are located on the hand. So pay close attention while you're drawing, to make sure that you are emulating what you see.

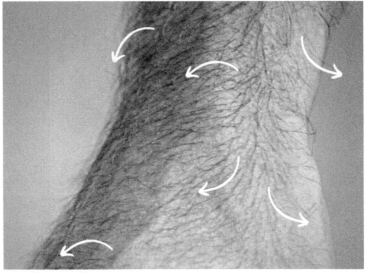

Note the directionality of the hairs at different places.

The hairs are also curved, all of them! I never noticed that before I really lasered in on the details like this.

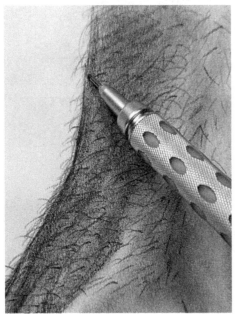

To get the look of the "downy" underlayer, use a mechanical pencil to make a lot of light, slightly curved strokes all over.

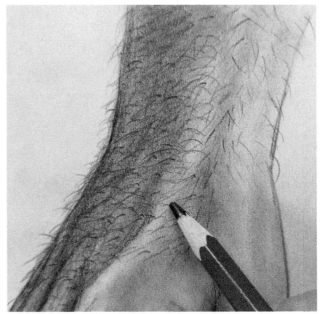

To achieve the top of layer of coarser hair, use your soft B pencil. Start out strong at the base of each hair and flick your pencil to make the short, curved stroke.

Now if ever there was time for a party, it's at the completion of this book! GREAT JOB! If you prefer learning from videos, I invite you to come learn with me online. I have recorded lessons for each lesson in this book and you can access them by joining my **Fun Fab Drawing Club at AwesomeArtSchool.com.**

For a low monthly fee, you get instant access to hundreds of hours of my real-time drawing lessons. You can then stream or download to watch at your leisure. It's basically Netflix, but for art nerds! My focus is primarily on creating fun portraits (both realistic and whimsical), and figures but we also dabble in urban sketching, perspective, drawing the decades, and more! There are new lessons added every month!

To add your name to the waitlist to be notified when registration opens, visit **awesomeartschool.com and click on Fun Fab Drawing Club WAITLIST**

Did you love this book?
If so, please consider letting others know with an Amazon review!

Thank You!

Fun Fab Drawing Club

Awesome Art School

Become the artist
you were born to be!

Let's Get Social

 awesomeartschool.com

 karencampbellartist.com

 facebook.com/karencampbellartist

 instagram.com/karencampbellartist

 youtube.com/karencampbellartist

 amazon.com/author/karencampbell

About the Author

Karen Campbell is a multi-media artist living in North Carolina with her computer geek husband, three kids, and 2 cats and Maggie the dog who thinks (like all dogs) she's hooman.

She is the proud founder of AwesomeArtSchool.com and the author of many books on drawing and mixed media.

Karen posts free weekly art tutorials on drawing and mixed media on her YouTube channel every Friday.

To find out more about her books, online classes, in-person workshops and annual Scottish Castle retreat, visit karencampbellartist.com.

More Books from Karen

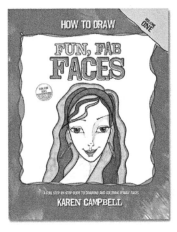

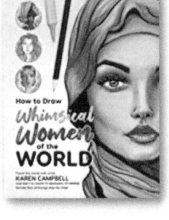

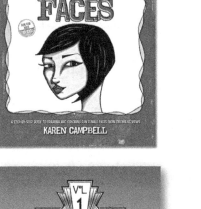

More on the Way!

Made in United States
Orlando, FL
02 February 2024

43079381R00091